To Nick,
Safe Diving!

Great Ocean Adventures

rom the five and
Animal Planet series
association with Scubazoo

Monty Halls

Great Ocean
Adventures

www.fullcircleexpeditions.com
The organization that co-ordinates these round the world diving expeditions.
If you fancy having a go at this trip yourself, these are the guys to sort it out
for you.

www.scubazoo.com
What can I say about Scubazoo? The bees knees in underwater filming terms.

Dedication

This book is dedicated to my mum and dad who, despite
overwhelming evidence to the contrary, remained convinced
that my errant wanderings around the world would amount to
something, and were supportive and encouraging throughout.

© 2007 Monty Halls

Published by Broadcast Books
on behalf of Full Circle Expeditions
84 Whiteladies Road, Bristol BS8 2QP
catherine@broadcastbooks.co.uk
www.broadcastbooks.co.uk
Tel: 0117 923 8891

Designed by Martin Laurie
martinlaurie@ukonline.co.uk
Tel: 01925 757 864

Illustrations © 2007 Patsy Breach

Printed and bound by
Bath Press, Lower Bristol Road, Bath

Isbn: 978 1 974092 54 4

Acknowledgements

So many people have helped me out in the making of the series and the writing of this book, it's impossible to know where to start. A big thank you to all the dive operators who hosted us, all great professionals, respected in the industry, and thoroughly nice people. A massive thank you to the photographers who donated images. They did so for an absolute pittance, in the belief that the story was worth telling and out of sheer enthusiasm for the undersea world. I speak as a terrible underwater photographer when I say the ability to dive and take stunning underwater images is a very special talent indeed, and I've been very lucky to work with these guys. Thanks also to Oceanic, Suunto, and Fourth Element Dive Clothing. A big thank you to Catherine from Bristol Book Publishers, Martin who did the designs, and Anne Benn for handling the distribution. Thanks also to mum, dad, Pats, Russ, Antje, Bodders and Al Summerlad – where would I be without you chaps. Finally, thanks so much to everyone who helped us out on the road – the kindness of strangers is how we managed to pull this whole thing off. I owe you all a beer (possibly several).

Sketches:

The sketches in this book are done by my sister, Patsy Breach. It's all rather unfair, I simply described where we went and she drew these lovely images on a couple of wet Wednesday afternoons. I know I may be slightly biased, but if you need someone to illustrate a book, give her a call. At present she's an air traffic controller with the most valuable doodle pad in the world I'd say. Contact her on: patsy.breach@virgin.net

Contents

The Making of Great Ocean Adventures

The Making of Great Ocean Adventures

The Great Ocean Adventures television series is billed as one man's journey around the world seeking out the giant animals in the sea. This is, of course, complete nonsense, as everywhere I go I am accompanied by a film crew, all of whom work considerably harder than me the vast majority of the time. Being behind the camera and not in front of it, they get very little credit in the eyes of the viewer, and yet they are completely essential to the making of the show. There is also a considerable amount of work that goes into researching and organizing a global series such as this, with those responsible not even having the luxury of getting a good tan for all their hard work researching exotic destinations.

Behind it all are also the production company executives who have the faith to back the project, and the television channel commissioning executives who provide the money and the means to transmit the final shows around the world. Without Matthew Frank, the head of RDF Media, who not only put up with me babbling away at him in his office but also decided to invest some of his hard- earned cash, there would be no Great Ocean Adventures. Without Bethan Corney of Channel Five and Mark Wild of Animal Planet, both of whom showed great tolerance and faith as we found our feet, we would certainly not have reached the audience we did. Nick, Nodge, and Mark did a tremendous job in the editing suites, turning sows' ears into silk purses on a daily basis. A more agreeable bunch of blokes you couldn't hope to meet. And without Anat Dimant, our fearsome Production Manager in London, we would not have managed on the limited funds we had to pull off a remarkable journey. If I would offer one piece of advice, one lesson learned from the Great Ocean Adventure experience, drawn from a thousand encounters in different countries and different cultures, it's this. Make sure you never upset Anat.

But the final and most heartfelt tribute must go to the team on the road. These productions are not the glossy, multi-million pound affairs that one might imagine. Great Ocean Adventures manages on an absolute shoe string, using the cheapest flights, the latest connections at the darkest hours, and the briefest of stay in each country to try to find and film the animals. We as a team travelled the road for three months, were perpetually tired, frequently sick, often irritable, and occasionally frightened. However the entire travelling circus that was the Great Ocean Adventures film crew never once took their eye off the ball, remaining supremely driven and focused to produce the best series possible. Their enthusiasm infected everyone around them, and the results – certainly in pure filming terms – speak for themselves.

Foremost amongst the crew were the underwater cameramen from Scubazoo, endlessly driven to produce superb footage. A series such as this lives or dies by the quality of the underwater sequences, and Scubazoo never, ever let us down, driving themselves into a state of burbling exhaustion to ensure that the essence of the giant animals we encountered underwater was captured perfectly.

For the whole crew, it seemed that 'impossible' was the default setting at every location, something to be taken on and beaten into submission with a great rush of energy and unstoppable optimism.

It is therefore with great pleasure that I introduce my travelling companions for Great Ocean Adventures:

Alastair Blaine – (Assistant Producer/Sound)

Alastair is deeply eccentric, and there is every chance that he should be in some sort of home. The quintessential Englishman, he was completely unflappable, and had the most extraordinary work ethic. He performed not one but four jobs during the filming process, frequently doing several of them at the same time. As there was absolutely no time for sleep, he swiftly became a hollow-eyed, muttering loon, and yet he ploughed on resolutely. The absolute life and soul of the crew, he pretty much held everything together, and to watch Alastair work is to realise why Britain once had an empire. Every film crew should have one.

Simon Enderby – (Underwater cameraman)

Simon is an elemental force of nature, utterly driven to produce cracking underwater footage. He is a large chap, and being the resourceful son of a Norfolk pig farmer has one or two tricks up his sleeve. We once had a scrap, Simon and I, over a disagreement about a day's filming. I thought myself pretty handy prior to this dust up, being a rugsy tugsy ex-Royal Marine and all that. Simon won the fight by sitting on my head and refusing to get off until I said sorry. Quite simply the most motivated, energetic, tireless person I have ever worked with, and the finest diver ever to don fins, although he does tell rather long stories that don't really have an ending.

Jason Isley –
(Underwater cameraman/stills photographer)

Jason was with us for the Newfoundland, Brazil, Mexico, British Colombia and Norway phases. A stocky, powerful figure who likes warm water, it gave us all an opportunity to learn several new swear words when he first jumped into frigid Canadian seas. Jason is completely unflappable, a calm stoic presence who complements the more fiery Simon. They are the Frodo and Samwise of underwater filming. He is an extremely talented underwater photographer, and many of the images in this book are his. Jason never, ever, not even once, beat me at pool during the entire filming of the series, a fact that infuriates him and that he will doubtless deny.

Roger Munns –
(Underwater cameraman / stills photographer)

Roger was with us for the Tonga, Philippines, and Bali phases of the trip. He looks very much like a small boy, and is frequently handed in at Lost Property in major airports. Women love Roger, and wherever we went he was mobbed by panting matrons who wanted to whisk him away to do all manner of unpleasant things to him. Another terrific underwater photographer, he had an intensely annoying habit of rolling into the water, casually blatting away with the camera, and producing images of startling excellence. Infuriatingly talented.

The vast majority of images in the book from Tonga, Malapascua, and Bali are taken by Roger. He is an excellent free diver, and can make a single cylinder last a fortnight.

Karen Walsh – (Director/Camerawoman)

Karen had the misfortune to travel the world with four big hairy men who thought that talking about partial pressures, o-rings and decompression sickness made for an interesting conversation. She also did the whole thing carrying a very large camera indeed. She never gave up, and was fearless in some fairly intense filming situations (late at night amongst 1200 sweating fishermen on the docks in Mexico being one of the more memorable). She writes a humdinger of a script.

Helping us out in Scotland were Russ Breach, Dan Stephenson, Chris Holt, and Dan Burton. All the sort of chaps you'd want at your shoulder should the chips be down, explorers and adventurers one and all. But for an accident of time they'd all be striding a deck amidst a blizzard of cannonade and red hot grape, and nicking people's countries.

This harum-scarum, dashing, swash-buckling circle of the globe was one of the greatest experiences of my life. We met some truly extraordinary people, had an intoxicating whiff of mysterious cultures, and were humbled by encounters with gigantic shadows in the open sea. I hope this book provides a small taste of the Great Ocean Adventures experience.

Chapter 1

The Mysterious
White Whale

Newfoundland and Hudson Bay

The Beluga Whale

The Mysterious White Whale – The Beluga

I realized that I liked Canada a great deal as I sat outside the customs office in Newfoundland Airport. One of the perpetual hazards of traveling with huge amounts of filming and diving gear is the assumption made by anyone in a uniform that a) you have something to hide, and b) you have a great deal of money. Neither is true of course, but the sight of vast mounds of equipment accompanied by a shifty looking, very tired camera crew seems irresistible to most customs officials, their beady little eyes inevitably lighting up the moment you come trundling through the green channel.

Previous page
Exploring the ghostly skeleton of a whale off the Newfoundland coast

True to form we had been waved aside as we wheeled several large trolleys through the airport, and were now sitting waiting as the customs officer laboriously went through our paperwork in his office. Shifting in an uncomfortable bucket seat like a bored teenager, I suddenly saw a tall and strikingly attractive girl walk round

the corner. Two things immediately grabbed my attention – the first was that she was wearing a customs officers uniform, the second was that she was carrying a huge tray of coffee and doughnuts.

The Arctic sun rising over the tundra.

"Hey guys" she said, revealing perfect white teeth that were a monument to the Canadian dental system, "I saw you sitting here looking kind of tired, and thought you might like some drinks and doughnuts."

I instantly liked Newfoundland immensely. I could have subsequently been mugged by ten lumberjacks and chased by a bellowing moose, and yet after that initial introduction I think I still would have liked it. First impressions do count you know.

Newfoundland is a beautiful, craggy, wild lump of rock moored precariously on the north eastern coast of Canada. It is perpetually battered by muscular swells, and trembles in the teeth of a freezing cold current that barrels down from Polar waters from what little remains of planet earth to the north. It's a wild rugged place

alright, but very beautiful, and we were all excited at the prospect of beginning the new series in such a wild location. Our target was the mysterious white whale, so vocal it is sometimes called the canary of the seas – the beluga.

Newfoundland has been the home of seafaring men and women for centuries, the reason being the hugely abundant fish stocks that fill these icy waters. The early Irish settlers called Newfoundland "Tam an Iskh" – the Land of the Fish, and the accents of the locals still carry the echo of their ancestors. Fishermen from Ireland and Cornwall made the perilous trip to the distant fishing grounds to the west, gradually pushing further and further into the Atlantic until the great cliffs of Newfoundland loomed above them. Many decided to stay, and they live on in every sentence uttered by the locals, a memory of home in every rounded vowel and delicious West Country burr.

The island is famous for its dense sea fog, a result of the combination of the frigid waters of the Labrador current hitting warmer water coming from the south, as well as the warmth from the land mass of the island itself. Combine these spiralling mists with the imposing dark cliffs that surround Newfoundland, and the place has the feel of fortress, with the sea dashing itself furiously against the battlements in great explosions of spray.

We were in Newfoundland not only to see the beluga whales. A significant whaling industry has been a mainstay of Newfoundland's economy until as recently as 1993, when a blanket ban finally put an end to the remnants of the whaling fleet. Humpback and fin whales move through these waters on their annual migrations, and awaiting them for the last couple of hundred years have been the ingenuity, the harpoons, the machinery, and the insatiable

Opposite: A local settlement looms out of the Newfoundland sea mist.

hunger of man. The animals we were hoping to encounter had been swimming into a two hundred year ambush that had only been called off a decade earlier – a one-sided massacre that saw the death of tens of thousands of whales. Populations of the whales are rebuilding slowly, but what thoughts stir in the minds of the older animals as they hear the low throb of a boat's engine? One can only begin to imagine.

As well as an embarrassing abundance of big animals in the sea, Newfoundland doesn't do too badly on land either. Much of the island is shrouded in dense forest, home to moose, elk, all manner of smaller mammals, and of course bears.

We had become peculiarly transfixed on the bears, and were quietly convinced that one of us would be dragged off into the murky gloom of the forest to be consumed at leisure by a snuffling grizzly. As we drove from the airport towards the coast, the discussion turned to suitable tactics should one encounter a bear. This in turn led to a range of half-baked and highly dubious pearls of wisdom that we had each picked up on our travels or on some of the ropier satellite documentaries: play dead, don't play dead, climb a tree, never climb a tree, run away, don't run away, fight back, never, ever, under any circumstances fight back.

I mentioned to Alastair that the one thing I was sure of was that making lots of noise when walking was a good idea, the idea being that the bear hears you coming and gets out of the way. I suggested the perfect kit for a walk in the wild Canadian woods was a compass, lots of water, and a one-man-band outfit of which you are furiously playing every instrument.

"Why's that?" asked Alastair, looking worried.

"Well, I don't know much about bears, but at least that way they know you're coming and you don't surprise one. I know they don't like surprises."

"Really? Birthdays must be a nightmare."

Thankfully the conversation was cut short by our arrival at Port St. John, our base for the week. Port St. John is quite beautiful, chocolate box pretty with clapperboard houses nestled on the shoulders of the steep hills that plunge into the estuary. We manhandled gigantic bags out of the taxi as we parked in the drive of our hosts – Ocean Quest Divers – and exchanged enthusiastic hellos with the boss Rick Stanley, a jocular, ruddy figure with an accent that should really have been bellowing directions from a foc'sle whilst bearing down on a sprinting whale.

With no time to waste, we piled our gear into the waiting van and hurtled down to the harbour, babbling and squabbling like an excitable school outing. This was our first destination, and no matter how experienced a film crew may be, the blood always races as the gear is unpacked for the first time.

This is one of the few places in the world where entering the water alongside beluga whales is permitted, and there was a tangible sense of excitement at the prospect of encountering one of the most charismatic of all the whales. Belugas are not large by whale standards, with a maximum length of about sixteen feet. But what they lack in size, they certainly make up for in charisma. Dark grey when born, they turn pure white at about ten years of age. They have a small head with a huge rounded forehead – known in whale science circles as a melon. This is used to considerable effect, focusing and condensing a vast range of chirps, clicks, whistles and squeaks. In days of yore, when men set sail in creaking wooden vessels on voyages of unimaginable hardship, in certain latitudes the voices of the belugas would resonate through the wooden hulls. To listen to these songs was said to drive a man to madness, and so the legends of the Sirens of the Sea was born – evil spectres that would draw a man to his death in the icy embrace of polar waters.

Nothing could be further from the truth, for the final endearing characteristics of the beluga is a particularly gentle and curious nature accompanied by an uncanny range of facial expressions. They also have a flexible neck, and will approach anything that arouses their curiosity (which is pretty much anything they come across) and peer at it from all angles, foreheads furrowed.

Rick seemed rather quiet as we moved out of the harbour. He was plainly biding his time, and eventually he gave a small cough and idly mentioned that not too many belugas had been seen so far this year. In fact, counting all the sightings from various outposts around the island, as well as data from research vessels, there had been a total of .....erm......ahhh......none.

Understandably this was met with something of a stunned silence, however after our initial disappointment, we swiftly rallied. All was in fact far from lost, as Newfoundland had some splendid diving, and the humpback whales were just arriving to feed on capelin – a small, silver, fish much like a herring that appears in vast numbers along the coast this time of year. The whales know this of course, and have been turning up for thousands of years to make the most of this annual bounty. They come from their breeding grounds in the Caribbean, and – not having eaten for four months – are a tad peckish on arrival. This presented a great opportunity to enter the water with them and watch one of nature's giants in action, sweeping up entire shoals of glittering fish in the massive expanding bellows of their throats, consuming swimming pool-sized lumps of the sea at a time.

The idea was to have a quick dive before looking for the whales, taking in some local reefs and a couple of wrecks. Rick steered us to the lee of a dark imposing cliff, looking for all the world like some mysterious Skull Island from a black and white movie set.

The fish shoals were certainly present, apparent in the plump seabirds dotting the ocean around us. Gannets, auks, shearwaters and gulls sat on the surface of the water, gorged with fish, glassy-eyed with gluttony. Best of all were the puffins, many of whom had eaten so much that they could no longer fly. Instead they would hop, skip, and flap from wave crest to wave crest as we approached in the boat, to eventually plough into a wave and sit with a "oh-run-over-me-then-I'm-too-full-to-care" expression on their painted faces. After these short sprints you could clearly see them panting.

"That's probably why it's called a puffin" noted Alastair, staring at one particularly plump bird.

My overwhelming feeling of excitement on kitting up and finally getting in the water was rudely shattered the moment my neoprene sheathed buttocks hit the surface. The water was 1°C, which is 32°F in imperial, or painfully cold in any other language. It shimmers and pulses with cold, and even the fish swim round looking pinched and pained. My full face mask, never my absolute favourite piece of kit, was subjected to a blast of invective unprecedented in any previous dive, causing it to steam up immediately, either from the force of the obscenities or the visor-cracking cold.

Water conducts heat away from the body many times faster than air, and I could almost feel the warmth seeping from my trembling frame. This is a factor that whales, being mammals, have also had to learn to deal with, so the evolutionary survival shop has equipped them with thick layers of blubber. This is a wonderful insulator, with a massive animal such as a bowhead whale, which lives most of its life in freezing Polar waters, having a layer of blubber about eighteen inches thick. This gives them a near circular physique, and they plough through the ocean like a gigantic beer barrel. Such is the efficiency of the blubber that a bowhead gives out the same amount of heat over its entire body as a 40 watt lightbulb. When chased (sadly an all-too familiar occurrence throughout the last century) the bowhead has to open its mouth to allow water to rush over its tongue to cool it down, the alternative being the massive muscles generating enough heat to essentially cook the whale in it's own blubber, a moderately unpleasant way to go I should imagine.

People – or certainly most people – lack the eighteen inches of blubber required to stay perfectly warm, and as such mankind has developed the drysuit. This certainly does the job, trapping a warm layer of air between the skin and the water, aided by what is essentially a giant romper suit termed a "woolly bear". This still leaves the hands and face exposed though, and to replicate the feeling of that first dive, one simply needs to do the following. Lower yourself into a large freezer amply stocked with tubs of ice cream. Furiously spoon the ice cream into your slack jaw, thus creating an ice cream headache of apocalyptic intensity. Then insert your fingers into a vice, and tighten the ratchet one click at a time. Continue to do both of these things until you have achieved a puckered gurn and you are drooling and trembling. You may now leave the freezer. Repeat three times daily for the complete diving experience.

Happily all of this discomfort was well worth it, as the diving was really very good indeed. This was certainly not your shimmering tropical reef, but nonetheless the reason this island has been so beloved of fishermen through the ages became apparent very swiftly. Lobsters peered from every sliver of darkness on the reef wall, whilst sculpins stared at me wide-eyed from their ambush positions. The sculpin is essentially a scorpion fish, and seems to consist mostly of a great armoured head, which in itself seems to be made up entirely of two gigantic eyes. These peer at you as you pass, moving independently of each other. This is a neat evolutionary touch allowing the sculpin to track two prey items simultaneously. However it is strangely disconcerting when you are the object under scrutiny, one eyed fixed firmly on you with a gimlet gaze, the other slowly scanning the middle distance for dinner.

Jason and Simon enjoying 1 degree celsius.

The aim of this first dive was actually to explore the wrecks of two whaling vessels, slowly giving themselves up to the sea and in the process becoming, in a nicely ironic touch, havens for marine life. The two wrecks lie close together on the sea floor, almost touching, and as I drifted over them I could still make out the dreadful efficiency of their sleek lines. With pistons thundering and their elegant prow slicing through the waters surface, this was a predator the whale simply had no answer for, and it was very nearly their undoing. It is always a source of amazement to me that given our history of gunning down the whale, they tolerate us today in the water with such grace and curiosity. Given their intelligence and capacity for learning, as well as recent evidence that they may live for up to 200 years, we should feel fortunate that they seem to be gentle creatures with little capacity for revenge. Were it otherwise there would be very little point in any of us ever entering the water at all.

Our first dive completed, we turned for home, crossing the open sea of a wide bay to travel back to Port St. Johns. As we crossed the open water, the most remarkable thing happened. Steaming into the cold air sitting above the water, somehow threatening and sterile with its frigid whiff of ozone and salt, we suddenly hit the warm air barreling off the land. We were still several miles out to sea, and yet the smell enveloped us, with the sweet whiff of conifers combining with the fuggy damp of grass and mud. For the fishermen and sailors who had battled mountainous seas over icy currents, this smell must have been like life itself. It was a wonderful moment, and we all glanced at each other and immediately smiled in recognition.

The next day we moved to the centre of whaling operations in this region, a town built entirely from the income of the flesh of thousands of whales. Its intense link with the sea is apparent in the name of the town itself – a traditional word denoting the two pieces of dowel used to hold oars in place in a dory. This in itself is rather quaint, and perhaps a matter of eyebrow-raising interest for the amateur historian. Time has, however, been somewhat unkind to this particular word, and sadly this settlement's name now rings less of a hard day at sea, and rather more of a quiet night in at home.

As we entered Dildo, the air was filled with muffled tittering from Alastair, Jason and Simon in the back seat of the cab. I turned to Karen and mentioned that we would have to do something about this – I simply couldn't do repeated pieces to camera about this place without feeling like I was in a second rate Carry On film. After a quick improvised production meeting, we satisfied ourselves with a walk past the main sign with me looking thoughtful and muttering something about traditional names, feeling all the while like Sid James.

Our home for the week. Monty shows his considerable maturity.

I thought it best not to mention that the next town along is called Spreadeagle.

Dildo was the home to the only whaling museum on the island, full of memorabilia from the bloody heyday of whaling. The guide around the museum was himself an ex-whaler, and showed me his diary from his days hunting the great whales as they hove into view each spring. Now an old man, his rheumy blue eyes misted over as he recalled the chase, a finger as gnarled and twisted as a piece of driftwood tracing the words on the page. He now works – as do many of the traditional whaling families in Newfoundland – in whale watching, taking groups of tourists out to see the whales as they roll in the lee of the cliffs around the island. He was a decent man, occupied as we all are with putting food on the table and providing an income for his family. He seemed entirely reconciled to his new life since the whaling ban, but occasionally as he talked of standing on the plunging bow of a whaling vessel at full speed, spray kicking and engines bellowing at the height of the chase, his eyes said otherwise.

The next three days in Newfoundland were spent in the fruitless pursuit of whales who would be prepared to come over and have a look at me as I hung in the water. This is a characteristic of young whales – imbued with the same level of curiosity as any other young animal – and adult whales whilst at leisure. The humpbacks this year had appeared slightly late in Newfoundland's waters, and wanted to do one thing – feed. They viewed our boat in much the same way as one would view a wasp at a picnic – an irritant to be avoided whilst the food was consumed.

We finally admitted defeat, having peered hopefully into the murk for the hundredth time, watching a great dark body power itself into the middle distance. Sadly we would have to search elsewhere, and our thoughts turned to the far north.

However before we left Newfoundland we had to be "screeched in" – another Newfoundland tradition. This was organized with considerable relish by Rick, and essentially seemed to involve drinking rum whilst a large man hit us over the head with an oar as his mates bayed him on. It struck me as one of those initiation ceremonies made up on the spot, but after eight years in the marines and lots of rugby clubs, the entire thing seemed to be a pretty good night out as far as I was concerned.

Our continuing quest for the belugas then took us (slightly) west and (a long way) north to the tiny community of Churchill on the shores of Hudson Bay. Although this is unquestionably the finest location on earth to see belugas, as we landed the people of the town were dealing with a more pressing seasonal problem. As it was spring, the ice to the far north of Hudson Bay had begun to melt, and in time-honored tradition, the polar bears that had been stalking the ice for seals had swum south to land on the rocky shores outside Churchill. They have been doing this for a very long time indeed, and I can only assume that the original settlers in Churchill had arrived in the midst of winter and decided it was as good a place as any to build a community. Glancing through

The local supermarket.

the curtains in Spring that first year would have brought forth an audible "Oh dear" as several hundred of the largest land carnivores on the planet landed on the shore 200m away from the town, and ambled towards the huts looking for buns. It's a problem the locals have learned to live with, although they do have a somewhat hunted expression, and ensure that no house or car is ever locked so there's somewhere to dart into when pursued by half a ton of galloping fur ball.

There hadn't actually been a death from a polar bear attack for twenty years in Churchill, and even then the unfortunate chap in question had rather stacked the odds against himself. In fact, if a panel of experts sat down and attempted to come up with the ultimate polar bear lure, they probably would have arrived at the figure that stumbled out of the ruins of a burnt-out hotel one dark night in 1986.

The victim was a local man with a pronounced limp. Having drunk himself senseless, he recalled in the dimmest part of his fogged brain that a local hotel had recently burnt down. Weaving his way to the smouldering ruins, he found what remained of the freezer, and having had a good old rummage, chanced upon a mound of fresh(ish) raw hamburger meat. Transporting the hamburger meat home would have presented problems had he not happened to have deep and generous pockets. He gleefully stuffed them full of dripping meat, until he resembled the polar bear equivalent of meals on wheels. Now there was the slight issue of the two mile journey home, a problem compounded by the fact that taxis were not available at this time of year, and there were no friends around to give him a lift. The obvious option was to walk – or rather stagger and limp – home through the darkness, surrounded by extremely hungry polar bears. The miracle is that he made it as far as he did.

Like the polar bears we had our own powerful reasons for being in Churchill, centred around a glorious scrum of white bodies jostling for position in the mouth of the Churchill River. Around 2,000 belugas mass in the river at this time of year, drawn by huge schools of capelin and the fact that the river is a positively tepid 10°C. This gives the young belugas a very good chance of survival, and also keeps them out of the reach of polar bears. Most adult belugas have scars on their backs, each a silent testimony to a moment of overwhelming terror as a great taloned paw crashed through the water's surface from above. The bears wait around gaps in the ice, and as the belugas surface to breathe they haul them onto the snow in what must be titanic battles.

Simon and Monty let loose on the only compressor in Churchill. The Health and Safety Executive may find the following scenes disturbing.

Our first glimpse of the elusive beluga.

So this was it, unequivocally my final opportunity to encounter a beluga in the water. As we moved out of the tiny harbour in a puttering inflatable boat, it seemed all of our dreams had been answered. In the middle of the river was a mass of white bodies, twisting and turning on the surface, rolling and snowy white in the leaden Arctic sun.

It seemed relatively simple – surely slipping over the edge of the boat would reveal a glorious pirouetting mass of white whales as far as the eye could see? Sadly, as soon as I entered the water I knew we were in all sorts of trouble. There is a very good reason why the whales have developed sonar and echo location, hunting as they do in near zero visibility under the ice. Although my ears told me in no uncertain terms that the whales were all around me, bombarding me with whistles and chirps like a frantically twiddled wireless, my eyes saw only impenetrable brown murk. It was pre- cisely as though I had gingerly lowered myself into a large vat of oxtail soup.

Our guide, however, had a few tricks up his sleeve, plainly having dealt with trembly-lipped, crushingly disappointed divers before. Seated by the outboard, he wordlessly began to rub his sou-wester- clad bottom back and forth along the rubber hull of the boat, producing a piercing set of squeals and squeaks. Glancing at me, he nodded his head back towards the water, and I meekly slipped back in.

Although the cacophony of bum and boat related noises meant very little to us, they plainly said something extremely compelling in beluga. As I peered into the murk, abruptly a white face appeared before me, ghost-like in the gloom, drawing back instantly leaving only a swirl of suspended particles, like fog on a moor. The squeaks resonating through the hull increased, as the bum sawing backwards and forwards above me went into overdrive. Again the face appeared, this time more slowly, a fifteen foot whale with his nose virtually pressed to mine. The whale angled his head, first one way then the other, peering at me with intense curiosity. I stared back, overwhelmed by the proximity of the animal, my facial expression a blank canvas compared to the beluga's.

Opposite The most enigmatic of all whales gives me a smile.

The moment the team realize they have the shot.

It is widely acknowledged that belugas can show a considerable range of emotions through expressions, and just before melting back into the darkness of the river and its own world, the whale gave me one last long look, head held at a distinctly quizzical angle, mouth curled in what looked for all the world like a smile.

Chapter 2

The Acrobat from the Forbidden Isle

Brazil

The Spinner Dolphin

The Acrobat from the Forbidden Isle –
The Spinner Dolphin

Dolphins are something of a banker for television companies, and the executives at *Channel Five* and *Animal Planet* had been keen that we include a dolphin encounter in at least one of our programmes. The problem was how to remain faithful to our sworn agenda – that we would operate off the beaten track and introduce the viewer to experiences and animals beyond the realm of normal travel shows. The title of the series was *Great Ocean Adventures*, and this could hardly be justified by paddling with Flipper off a beach packed with day trippers. So we set about tracking down obscure dolphin encounters with a near missionary zeal.

It is at moments such as this that fate frequently lends a subtle hand. After an inordinate amount of pencil sucking and chin scratching over several weeks, we had still not come up with a good dolphin angle. One evening at home I decided to take a bath, and, retiring

Previous page
The tiny port at
Fernando de Noronha.

40

to the tub, I was accompanied as ever with the key constituents of the complete bathing experience. This included a bottle of fragrant bubble bath, a travel magazine, and an excellent glass of white wine. Without wishing to betray my hard man credentials, there really is no finer experience than emerging from the bathroom after a long soak, slightly light headed, having read a humdinger of an article, and carrying the faint whiff of summer fruits. I confess this was not something I mentioned during my original interview so many years before with the Royal Marines when asked about favourite past-times – I believe I enthused about fell running in Y-fronts and wrestling heifers.

After settling into a bath so hot it created a plimsol line of scalded flesh, I opened the magazine, and there it was. A tiny editorial piece on a Brazilian fishing village called Laguna, where rumour had it the dolphin population hunted in unison with the local fishermen. Moments later a trail of damp footprints meandered down the stairs, leading to a perspiring figure on the phone ringing my only Brazilian friend for more information. The subsequent

Sunset off Fernando de Noronha.

conversation saw the planets of the television universe neatly align, as my friend also told me of a mysterious island off the coast where the largest resident pod of spinner dolphins in the world were said to live. Acrobatic dolphins off a forbidden island and an extraordinary co-operation with man – we had our programme.

Several weeks later saw us landing at the airport in Florianopalis, the capital of the southern Brazilian state of Santa Catarina. Our camera crew could be described as many things, but "easy on the eye" is probably not one of them, having slightly too many paunches and bald spots to be considered calendar material. This was immediately thrown into stark contrast as we walked through the airport, surrounded as we were with olive skinned, raven haired beauties. Brazil is essentially a giant catwalk, and must have more beautiful women per capita than any other country on earth. To compound our pale, saggy discomfort yet further, Florianopolis is famed as being the city with the most attractive women in the whole country. The first woman I saw was a snake hipped, brown eyed vision of health and vitality that swept passed on roller blades, dazzling us all with a smile as she vanished into the middle distance. I thought that she was part of some sort of promotion or publicity stunt, however Alastair pointed out that she was in fact an airport cleaning lady. It was really at this point that I realized that Brazil was going to be a slightly different experience from other destinations.

Sure enough, as we drove south to the small town of Laguna, we soon had our faces pressed to the windows of the cars like kids in a safari park. Tiny bikinis, pert bottoms, perfect bosoms, and raven hair abounded. And you should have seen the women.

We duly arrived in at the tiny coastal community on the outskirts of Laguna that was to be our home for our short visit. Arriving

Opposite
Spinner dolphins are built for speed and agility.

– as ever – in darkness, we moved our gear into a series of neat haciendas tucked into the dunes at the back of a great sweep of beach, before being lulled to sleep by the chirping of cicadas and the roar of Atlantic breakers.

We awoke to a beautiful dawn, and the sight of one of the most famous surf beaches in Brazil. Explosions of spray accompanied the percussive arrival of massive waves pounding a wild arc of beach, with the tiny figures of surfers twisting and gyrating in their midst. The temptation to join them was strong, however we were gently advised by our hosts that we should stay on dry land, as the locals took a dim view of incompetent tourists carving up their waves. Numerous tales abounded of surprised visitors receiving some impromptu dental work under a flurry of tanned fists in the local car park, and so we trooped of to breakfast instead.

It was a short drive to Laguna, in itself a fascinating little town. Colonised by the Portuguese in 1676, the community had recently taken it upon itself to restore 600 of the original buildings to their colonial splendor. This has been done out of a sense of civic pride and, unusually for our commercially orientated eyes, no further attempts had been made to court tourism. The town consists of sleepy squares and ancient taxis rumbling over cobbled streets. The beach where the fishermen work with the dolphins is a non-descript stretch of sand and mud, and we would have driven straight past had our guide not pointed it out.

The fishermen are fiercely protective of their dolphins, and are said not to like outsiders disrupting a routine that has been in place for over 150 years. As such we respectfully set up our cameras a considerable distance back from the shore and watched the spectacle unfold in front of us.

What we were about to witness had been recorded as far back as the first century by the Romans, and yet today takes place in only two places on earth – here in Laguna, and in a tiny fishing village in West Africa. Such is the local reliance on the dolphins that should they not appear, the fishermen do not even bother to turn out. There is a real intensity in the relationship between dolphin and man here in Laguna, so much so that each animal is given a specific name. One such animal – called Galha Torta – was so famous that when we asked one fisherman who was better known, Galha Torta or Pele, his brow furrowed and he took several moments to answer.

"About the same" he finally said, obviously delighted in his diplomatic answer.

Considering that football is followed with tribal fervour throughout Brazil, and that Galha Torta died in the late 1960s, for a bottlenose dolphin that is not bad going.

The brightly coloured fishing boats were lined parallel to the shore in front of us, each with a single fishermen standing in it peering out towards the mouth of the estuary. A distinct stir went through the boats as the first glistening back of a dolphin broke the surface in the distance, with a small pod of them coursing back and forth across the estuary like great sheep dogs. Driving a school of panicking fish before them, the dolphins headed directly towards the line of boats. As the fish reached the boats, the dolphins would suddenly surface, rolling and splashing, with several even eyeing the fishermen directly in an unmistakable signal to cast the nets. The fishermen would hurl their nets in a sweeping, glistening arc towards the fish. As they hit the water some of the fish would flee back towards the open water, and straight into the line of

One group of fishermen in Laguna wait for the other group of fishermen to turn up for work.

waiting dolphins. As a demonstration of perfect teamwork it was devastating, with the fish the victims of a co-operative effort that had been refined over generations of both man and dolphin.

During a momentary lull in the action, one of the fishermen abruptly turned and beckoned me forward.

"You try," he said with commendable brevity, handing me thirty pounds of soaking nylon net. After a brief demonstration of how to cast the net, he sat back and lit a cigarette with what can only be described as a look of delighted anticipation. I couldn't help noticing that the activity in the other boats had also stilled, with several stubbled faces turned in my direction.

It seemed relatively simple. Hang on to the net with both hands, and grip the edge between the teeth. When prompted by a snorting dolphin, hurl net in wide sweeping arc, thus enfolding the shoal of speeding fish. What could be simpler? As the dolphins swept ever closer, my heart rate increased, and my breathing quickened. Glancing at the fisherman – Eduardo – I could see that he had now sat up, and although not quite rubbing his hands together in glee, was certainly looking forward to the arrival of the shoal at the edge of the boat.

Suddenly the water in front of me was filled with darting silver shapes, and a grey back rolled and splashed just out of range of the net. All reason and logic fled my brain, and I twisted like a discus thrower, hurling the net with an explosive grunt of effort. It span out ahead of me in a massive arc, spray spinning from its rim, unfolding in a great circle.

I should remind anyone reading this that when throwing a net for the first time it really is extremely important to twist the body, throw upwards, and let go with both hands simultaneously. However, most crucial of all is to let go with the teeth. Sadly, this was the one thing that escaped me at the key moment.

Should that moment have been frozen in time, it would have seen a grown man with eyes bulging in surprise, teetering in a small boat, the tendons of his unnaturally extended neck standing out like hawsers, and thirty pounds of frisbeeing fishing net gripped firmly

The moment when the nets are prepared to be cast.

between his teeth. There was a heart-stopping moment when I nearly overbalanced, facing the unpleasant prospect of hitting the water wrapped in yards of nylon net in the midst of a panicking fish shoal, and then a Herculean effort that saw me remain in the boat. I stood bewildered with the net still dangling from my lower jaw peering about me at the fishermen, who were now helpless with mirth. Even the dolphins were laughing.

The rest of the morning passed pleasantly enough, with the dolphins gradually losing interest in the hunt, and the fishermen following suit. With a twinkle in his eye and a quiet chuckle, Eduardo bade us farewell. The glistening pile of fish in the bottom of his boat showed that it had been a good days fishing, and what's more he had seen a splendid display of incompetence from a gangly tourist – all in all a rather good day on the beach for Eduardo. We left him smiling wistfully and gathering his nets.

Seconds from total humiliation. Note clenched jaw and Eduardo looking on in delight.

The Acrobat from the Forbidden Isle – The Spinner Dolphin

Filming in Laguna. It all starts to get to Al.

That night we were invited to a barbeque by our Argentinian hosts, who had moved to Brazil many years before. We were, of course, an English camera crew. The reason for mentioning this is that all three countries had been knocked out of the World Cup in the previous 24 hours, an apocalyptic event as far as everyone around us was concerned, so all in all we weren't expecting a wacky evening.

To our surprise and delight a South American barbeque consists of pretty much the entire hind quarters of an ox being lifted onto a raging fire, with bits being lopped off and then carried to your plate still twitching. It was a faintly primeval scene as we slavered and gobbled raw meat, the lights of the flames dancing off the blood and oil dripping down our chins. We wobbled our way back down the hill many hours later, with heaving bellies and fuzzy heads. As I drifted off with the noise of the surf enfolding me, I reflected that life simply doesn't get any better.

The next morning we began our journey to Fernando de Noronha. This tiny island group consists of 21 lumps of rock of varying sizes jutting through the surface of the Atlantic Ocean, 300km off the Brazilian coast. The islands have a chequered history, being seen as having vital strategic importance as a stepping stone to the New World. They have been occupied by the French, the Spanish and Portuguese, and spent much of their history as a penal colony. The vegetation of the islands has been stripped away and replaced in part by hardwood trees, planted because they do not float and prisoners could therefore not use them for rafts. Although this had a significant impact on the terrestrial life of the islands, beneath the waves it is a different story, and the islands are known as the

Fernando de Noronha, the most beautiful islands in the Atlantic.

Galapagos of the Atlantic. Like all oceanic islands, they are an oasis of life in the desert of the surrounding ocean, creating upwellings of nutrient-rich water that in turn draw in a dazzling array of marine animals.

The islands are now governed with a rod of iron by the Brazilian Government, which has imposed draconian rules in an attempt to save a unique ecosystem. Tourist numbers are strictly limited – with only 420 allowed on the island at any one time, and in late 2002, the United Nations declared the island group a World Heritage Site. Such overwhelming levels of protection have caused the locals to re-name Fernando de Noronha "The Islands of the Forbidden."

As we flew in, the volcanic origins of the archipelago were plain to see in the large rocky cone that dominates the largest island. This rock is said to look like a human penis, with two smaller rocks just offshore apparently looking like breasts. I couldn't see it myself, however I reflected that the chaps who discovered the island in the seventeenth century had spent months in a boiling wooden hull surrounded by sweaty men, and most things probably looked like boobs by then, although I imagine the guy who said "Yeah, and the thing in the middle looks like a giant willy" probably struggled to get someone to share the night watches with him from that point on.

We were met at the airport by our hosts, who piled us into several beach buggies for the short drive to their dive operation. There is essentially one road in Fernando de Noronha, a five kilometre strip of tarmac endlessly patrolled by the island's lone policeman, ever optimistic of catching someone speeding. He is periodically called upon to conduct an undercover operation, walking around the island in civilian clothes being cheerfully saluted by everyone, who of course know precisely who is. I get the impression that there are more fulfilling posts in the Brazilian police force.

We had only two days on the island, and as such quickly sorted our gear and headed to the dock and our waiting boat. We were only permitted a single dive with the spinner dolphins, and that was due to take place the next day. Happily there was at least one other dive we were determined to do. The Brothers are two huge rocks that break the surface approximately a kilometre offshore, and promise much in the fury and foam that surrounds them. Such sites channel tides and currents, drawing in food for smaller fish, which in turn attract larger predators. It had all the hallmarks of a classic dive site.

It was therefore only a couple of hours after touching down that we were heading out towards the Brothers, the boat pitching and rolling wildly in the Atlantic swells. On arrival at the rocks, the boat's engines stilled briefly, and we leapt overboard straight into the spin cycle of the wild water alongside the rocks. Driving hard for the sea bed fifty feet below, we got our first glimpse of life beneath the waves in Fernando De Noronha.

Five species of turtle and fourteen species of shark inhabit these shallow seas, and the densely colonized rock faces spoke volumes for the rich waters around us. Brightly coloured gorgonian sea fans jostled for positions with lurid sponges and encrusting organisms, whilst grouper and snapper passed overhead. All of this colour and movement was obliterated however, by the spectacle that slowly rolled in from the open ocean.

Sweeping towards us was the largest fish shoal I had ever seen. It rolled and pulsed like a massive storm front, taking on a life of its own, each fish a tiny cell contributing to the whole dark organism. The edges of the shoal were periodically splintered in attacks from schools of jack and barracuda, and yet nothing could stop its progress. It soon enveloped us, giving us the chance to identify the fish within as anchovy, spinning and rolling about us in clouds. Simon and Jason were lost in the midst of the shoal, sometimes only visible through the red eye of the camera light, recording every moment of one of nature's great spectacles. Fish shoal in this way to confuse and intimidate predators, and it was easy to see how the sight of such teeming multitudes can overwhelm and confuse. It was a glorious introduction to these mysterious islands, and as we reviewed the footage that evening the anticipation built for our dive the next day – our long awaited appointment with the spinner dolphins.

To give it its more precise name, the long snouted Spinner dolphin is a wonder even amongst the dolphin family. The most acrobatic of all the dolphins, spinners have been known to spin seven times along their longitudinal axis in explosive jumps that carry them ten feet into the air. This is thought to be a means of communication, although the jury is still out and many observers think it may simply be a sign of exuberance. Their acrobatic tendencies made them the obvious target for early dolphinariums, but spinners died quickly in captivity. This is an animal with a mass of muscle and power that needs the open ocean. The spinner would simply fade away in the echoing concrete box that passes as a tank in even the largest aquarium.

Fernando de Noronha is unique in that a very large resident pod of dolphins visits the island every day. At dawn the pod returns from

Simon in the midst of the mighty anchovy shoal.

the night's hunt, having spent the last few hours pursuing squid and fish in the open ocean. Great numbers move into the Baja de Dolfino to relax, play, mate and rest prior to moving back out to sea as the daylight fades. Up to 2,000 dolphins may use the bay at any one time.

Swimming with the dolphins in the bay is normally strictly forbidden. However I had been granted special permission to snorkel with them as they moved out of the bay to begin the hunt late in the day. We passed a tense morning preparing our gear, checking cameras, housings and dive gear a million times over. This was a one stop shop for us – if we failed there would be no second attempt permitted.

As we rocked at the entrance to the bay, the water beneath us was clear as Bombay Sapphire gin, giving the impression that the boat was floating in mid air. All we could do was wait, feet dangling in the water, the warm sun on our backs. The island shimmered in the middle distance, the great volcanic cone rising from its centre, the summit of a mountain the shoulders of which stretched away into the deep water beneath our keel.

Suddenly Simon rose to his feet, and wordlessly pointed into the distance. Rounding the point of the bay were the scouts of the main group of dolphins, moving at speed, breaking the water's surface and throwing up a brief spray of foam and droplets. In only moments they would be upon us, and the deck exploded into life as we threw on our gear.

Spinner dolphins operate in large pods, and have a distinct hierarchy. The males move ahead of the main group, investigating any threats or unusual objects in the water. As we lowered ourselves

gently into the clear water, we knew that we had to impress the lead animals if we were to have the magical encounters with the females and young that we knew would soon follow.

The clarity of the water allowed us to spot the lead animals very quickly. They arced into deeper water, passing beneath us and peering upwards. We hung motionless in the water – there is very little point in chasing a dolphin – and watched them disappear into the distance. Moments later they were back, this time a little slower, a group of five males checking out these strange visitors to their world.

The male spinner dolphins meet the boat as it enters the Baja de Dolfino.

The inspections slowly got closer and closer, until at one point I had to arch my back to avoid the lead male. There is a strict no touching rule in Fernando de Noronha, something that plainly no one has thought to mention to the dolphins. Dolphins communicate by posture as well as sound, and I twisted my body to mirror their movements, watching them come ever closer and look at me quizzically.

Glancing downwards, I made out a host of shapes against the white sand beneath me, and realized with a jolt that the females and young had been permitted to join the party. Once again their initial approach was cautious; however like all young animals the juvenile dolphins had to be quietly restrained by their mothers, breaking away time and time again from the main group to charge towards us, only to be headed off by increasingly frustrated adults.

After a stand-off of several minutes, the first youngsters at last broke through, and suddenly we were surrounded by the main part of the pod. This was the zenith of the encounter, with people and dolphins simply enjoying one another's company. The culmination came in the moment I dragged a piece of seaweed through the water, letting it fall behind me, only to have it gathered by the pectoral fin of a passing adult and then returned to me, the ultimate moment of acceptance.

The spinner dolphin is a remarkable animal, possessing an exuberance and athleticism beyond any other marine creature. Although there are always hard-headed scientific arguments to explain any form of animal behaviour, as the grey bodies of the dolphins twisted and pirouetted in the blue water around me in the shadow of a remote, forbidden island, for a brief moment they seemed to represent the freedom of the open ocean itself.

Opposite
Spinner dolphins in the blue water of the open ocean, where they unequivocally belong.

Chapter 3
The Red Devil

Mexico

The Humboldt squid

The Red Devil – The Humboldt squid

Behind the corridors of the Natural History Museum, teeming with tourists and hyperactive kids, lurk the real treasures. Slip through a side door, unlocked by a suspicious janitor who eyes your pass over the top of half moon specs, and one enters a silent world far removed from the madding crowd outside. Here are the vaults of the museum, where specimens are stored and filed, pinned out in trays or staring lifeless out of round glass jars. It is an Aladdin's cave for the amateur naturalist, a maze of tunnels and annexes that lead you on past endless wooden drawers labeled in sepia copperplate writing.

I had actually visited this part of the museum before. Many years previously I had been part of an expedition to Central America, seeking out insects in the clicking, seething murk of the rainforest. Prior to departure I had been taken on a tour of the museum by one of the scientists in the team, who had reverentially opened a drawer

Previous page
A squid fisherman off Santa Rosalia cuts up the nights catch.

60

Santa Rosalia in the late afternoon, the squid boats ready to depart.

at the back of one of the vaulted rooms. He pointed wordlessly to a label above a rank of pinned out beetles, frozen in time at the moment of escape. The label was completed in an elegant hand, letters finished with a glorious swirl of fading ink. Such was the elaborate nature of the writing that it took me a moment to make out the signature of a young Charles Darwin, making me start at the handwriting of the Father of Evolution, inches from my nose.

Today we were going to the very bowels of the museum, to one of the only rooms capable of housing the monster within. This was the starting point of one of the most hazardous of the films in our series, one I was viewing with a healthy level of trepidation. Begun in the Museum, the journey would culminate in pitch black water thousands of miles away, surrounded by the hurtling bodies of a master predator from another world.

We were here to see the largest preserved giant squid in the United Kingdom – which means it is slightly larger than the other one, as there are only two in the first place. This is not an animal that mankind encounters on a regular basis, which is just as well as it would make very short work of us indeed. Fortunately Mother Nature has decided that giant squid should inhabit the abyssal deep water beyond the continental shelf, about as far away from people as it's possible to be. Even the Latin name speaks volumes, *Architeuthis dux,* translating as The Ruling Squid, a good name for an animal that exists beyond both our technology and imagination. The average depth of the oceans is about two and half miles, and this is the domain of the giant squid, a world of almost complete darkness, so much so that many of the inhabitants have to produce their own light. The giant squid patrols the deep canyons and plains that dominate the vast majority of our planet's surface, a truly fearsome predator that swoops out of the darkness in a multi-armed ambush never directly witnessed by man. It is well equipped to operate in the gloom of deep water, having the largest eye of any living organism, a twelve inch orb the size of a car hub cap.

The giant squid in the tank was actually something of a disappointment on first inspection, a flaccid, twisted collection of peeling limbs and pale flesh. It was only on closer examination that the true grandeur of the animal was realized, in the savage hooks around each wicked sucker on the main club tentacles, in the siphon that had propelled this animal through the night sky of deep water, and in the great eye that peered from folds of flesh. Squid of all sizes tend to operate the same mode of attack – a fearsome rush at a prey item, a pause, then the two main club tentacles flying out to secure the prey with hooked suckers, dragging it towards the eight smaller arms to be enfolded and lacerated by the scissoring beak within.

Of course we were not going to see a giant squid – although such a sighting would create possibly the most memorable (and shortest) finale to a programme in television history, as our babbling presenter is dragged wide-eyed and wriggling to a deep canyon to be consumed at leisure. But we could come alarmingly close, and had decided to set out to encounter an animal with just as fearsome a reputation, the new boy on the predatory block who is only just drawing the attention of the diving glitterati – the Humboldt squid.

Even with extensive research we didn't know a great deal about the Humboldt squid. I knew its local name amongst fishermen in the Sea of Cortez is *Diablo Rojo* – the Red Devil. For many years it was feared above all other predators – sharks included. To fall into the sea with Humboldt squid present was thought to be instant death, a hideous thrashing demise in the unforgiving embrace of a creature from hell itself.

The reality is, as ever, slightly more prosaic. The Humboldt squid is indeed a highly efficient predator, hunting in packs of up to a thousand animals and investigating anything in its domain. Rising to the shallow water at night, they are now the mainstay of a thriving fishing industry, and much of their reputation is founded on their behaviour when caught on the end of a line and dragged into a boat. Much as you and I would, they tend to thrash about and try to bite the fishermen. Back in their own environment, recent evidence has emerged that they are intelligent hunters, with a certain level of co-operation, although cannibalism is also rife amongst them.

What is certain is that populations in the Sea of Cortez have exploded over the last ten years, thought to be due to the demise of the shark, the latter vanishing under the sustained assault of the shark fin fishing industry. The squid now fill the niche once occupied by the shark, and are the most successful predator in the region by some distance. They are also extending their range north at an alarming rate, appearing off-shore even in the cold waters of Alaska. This red predatory tide has a significant local impact wherever it appears, and there is considerable chagrin in the scientific world as to why the Humboldt squid has suddenly begun to dominate so many ecosystems. There are thought to be as many as 20 million Humboldt squid in the Sea of Cortez. For someone about jump into that same body of dark water, that represents an awful lot of arms and beaks.

Our plan was to enter the water with the Humboldt squid, and explore their reaction to a group of divers. We were by no means the first to do this, as there had already been a limited number of diving pioneers who had dived with the squid. The confusion came in the stories one heard about these dives. Some spoke of fearsome battles in the darkness, with squid grabbing mouthpieces and equipment, dragging flailing divers into deeper water. Others recounted tales of gentle exploration, of an animal blessed with intelligence and grace who carefully investigated any alien object in its realm. There was only one way to find out the truth, and that was to fly out to the Sea of Cortez, clamber into our kit, fumble-fingered with fear, take one last longing look at the moon, and then jump into the darkness.

Travelling to Mexico itself swiftly turned into a hideous epic. Although modern travel should mean being whisked from departure point to arrival in seamless comfort, sadly our limited budgets meant a series of low cost airlines and departures at ungodly hours. This places unique demands on the body, and invariably means that one arrives on location already exhausted, when of course the diving has to start. The fact that we were accompanied by 800kg of filming gear that had to be manhandled off and on various obscure modes of transport added immeasurably to the joy of the journey.

The trip from Heathrow to the tiny town of Santa Rosalia took three and a half days, and involved six flights, a six hour stay in a ropey little hotel en route (just long enough to give us all a vigorous bout of food poisoning), a four and a half hour queue in Mexico City Airport (a new personal record), neatly topped off by a two hour drive in searing heat along a shimmering ribbon of tarmac. We arrived absolutely exhausted in the small hours, and collapsed into our respective rooms.

The next morning saw sunlight streaming through my curtains at a lobotomizing intensity. On stumbling naked to the window, I got a huge shock on throwing open the curtains at the sight of the town that gasped in the heat before me. Not quite as large a shock as the small Mexican lady watering the hanging basket directly outside the window, but a shock nonetheless.

Santa Rosalia is a town like no other, as brutal a place I had ever encountered on any of my travels. It is a genuine frontier town, and shimmers in the heat of a canyon on the edge of the desert that makes up most of the Baja Peninsula. The town was established in 1885 by the French, centred around a local mining boom. The mine was an unimaginable, fetid hell, where men descended into the steaming heart of the earth to pick away at the ore within, four thousand of them dying in the process. The hotel we stayed in was straight out of the Wild West, and had been built in 1888. They had even thoughtfully provided some nineteenth century pornography for me, in the form of a sepia picture in my bathroom of a plump lady removing what can only be described as hosiery whilst glancing coquettishly at the camera.

The ore seams soon ran dry, and the mine closed in 1985. Santa Rosalia – already a harsh, relatively lawless collection of huts and

Outside the hotel, Monty leaking gently in sweltering heat.

bars – descended further into the mire. It became known as the House of the Devil, and was thought to be cursed, so much so that in the late eighties a priest was called to exorcise the entire town. Standing on a hill top, he conducted a service to throw out the demons. It seems they took up residence on the sea nearby, as the next year the first large numbers of squid started to be caught in the local waters, and the fishing industry in Santa Rosalia was born.

Nowadays over a thousand fishermen head out to sea each night, and return before dawn with about a quarter a million pounds of squid in their small boats. Their financial cut on the squid is tiny, and most of them only scrape a living. Essentially the docks seem to consist of several hundred bored, tired, underpaid fishermen armed with large filleting knives. It was into the midst of this stubbled throng that, shortly after our arrival, Alastair wandered on an adrenalin-packed trip to set up an interview that evening.

The first we knew of his little adventure was when Alastair re-joined us as we were setting up our gear in the hotel foyer. Pink with perspiration, he had what can only be described as a slightly hunted look in his eye as he walked wordlessly past us and ordered a large juice at the bar. Sitting on a stool, and pausing periodically to stare into the middle distance, he told his story. His initial attempts to set up the interview had involved chatting to a group of fishermen playing poker amid the stink and refuse of the dockside. They had watched him silently as he talked to them, his volume decreasing as their silence drew out, broken only by one of the fishermen picking up a knife to clean under his nails. Looking at Al through hooded eyes he said: "Nice watch you have there." Al had returned to the hotel in the classic "walking-fast-but-not-quite-running" gait of the troubled Englishman, and was now only contemplating a return to the docks accompanied by local guides and possibly some sort of heavy machine gun.

Thankfully my first appointment of the day was to be slightly less exciting, as it was with one of the leading experts on Humboldt squid in the world – Professor William Gilly. Far from being a lab-coated academic, Professor Gilly liked nothing more than being in the thick of things out on the water, hauling on lures and wading into thrashing holds on local boats to measure extremely annoyed squid. He was on his boat at the dockside when I arrived, tinkering with lines and fittings, cold beer to hand. He greeted me warmly

and waved me into a seat on the deck. Reaching into a vast cooler, he produced a cold beer and sat opposite me, virtually vibrating with enthusiasm at the prospect of discussing his beloved squid.

The world of marine biology is full of people like William Gilly, fanatics who are supremely driven to learn all they can about their chosen animal. Their work is frequently underfunded, unacknowledged, and often extremely dangerous, and yet every time I encounter the Professor Gillys of this world they seem to be some of the most supremely happy people you could ever meet.

The journey takes its toll on Monty and Jason, whilst Simon keeps an eye out for anything he can point a camera at.

"Aha, yes, the beast from the deep," said William, eyes crinkling. "This really is one of the most impressive predators on earth, you know. There has been an explosion in their numbers, and for me that is simply the occupation of a niche vacated by the sharks. It's quite fitting, really, they are such an adaptable and capable animal."

To illustrate his point, he reached into the same cooler that held the beer and with a grunt hefted out a very substantial, very dead, Humboldt squid. Laying it on a bait table at the stern of the boat, he chattered away before realizing that the film crew hadn't moved, and were motionless on the deck, staring at the squid, slack jawed and wordless.

Here was the nightmare made real, a creature we had encountered only in research and in glossy images, which had assumed mythical proportions in our minds. It was as if William had produced a minotaur from the fridge, swiftly followed by a unicorn from the main cabin.

He laughed, and beckoned us closer. We edged forward, all the while being watched by that dark eye, collectively wary as though the squid could still lash out with those fiery red tentacles. A delighted William ploughed on with his animated description of the squid, this time illustrated by lifting various portions of its anatomy and waggling them at us.

"You all know about the tentacles of course, but did you know that there are a total of 2,000 suckers, each ringed with 36 teeth. That's essentially 72,000 teeth per squid! There is also this of course."

Professor William Gilly moments before performing his party trick of producing a very large, very dead Humboldt squid.

He reached into the mass of tentacles, heaving them to one side and exposing a dark orb about the size of a tangerine in their midst.

"This is the beak," he said proudly, eyeing the squid as though he had raised it personally and it had recently graduated, "a truly remarkable weapon. It's made of chitin, with a hooked top part that overlaps the lower segment." With great difficulty he prised the beak apart, exposing wickedly sharp upper and lower mandibles.

"We think that the squid don't just bite something once, that in fact the beak operates by biting a great many times in quick succession. We have yet to conclusively measure the speed, but it looks as though it's several times a second."

The thought of diving into the midst of several hundred of these squid was becoming less and less attractive. It would be like being neatly diced by a flock of giant demented parrots.

"The final thing worthy of note is that we've only just discovered that the base of the tentacles have a fine web connecting them. I think this could be for gathering plankton. We're looking at an animal here that can operate at every level of the food chain, which probably explains how it can grow from larval stage to five or six feet in a single year."

The morning passed all too quickly, with William a highly entertaining and slightly eccentric companion. He plainly could have talked about the squid all day, and had an eerie collection of tales from many a moonlit night out on the Sea of Cortez. He told us of one night where the moon had been so bright that the squid had sculled up the from deep water in their thousands and, mesmerized by the light, had reached through the surface of the water as though trying to draw down the moon itself, surrounding his boat with a forest of waving tentacles bathed in a silver glow.

Our dive was to take place later that night, and soon we had to return to the hotel to prepare our gear. Taking our leave of Professor Gilly, leaving him happily up to his elbows in slime and glutinous tentacles, we walked back up the hill through the shimmering heat, gasping and stumbling. It is a wonder that anything lives here at all, and there is a general air of tough resolve throughout the town. Even the weeds look hard.

For Simon and Jason, there were all manner of technical preparations required to get their equipment ready to deal with a certain set of

Two entirely aquatic organisms – Simon and a sea lion – get acquainted. Simon is the one on the right.

diving conditions. Filters, lights, batteries, housings – all must be prepared meticulously. For me it was slightly simpler, laying out my dive gear and conducting a few simple checks, then packing it away. This left me several hours to lie on my bed, staring at the fan creaking in slow circles above me as it moved baking hot air in languid circles. As the sun slowly dipped towards the horizon, still a fierce red orb even as it was swallowed by the sea, I thought of the pulsing bodies in the dark water, beginning their meteoric rise through the water column to commence the hunt. Finally, as the last light slipped away and true darkness settled outside, I gathered together my kit and headed towards the waiting vehicle. It was now true night, the realm of the squid.

The film crew were quiet as we drove the short distance to the dock, all wrapped up in our own thoughts and wrestling with our individual fears. In my experience, people always change at night-time, the darkness awaking primeval fears and ancient instincts. We were all aware that we were heading into immensity of the Sea of Cortez to face a great predator in its own environment.

The boat was tugging at its mooring in the harbour like a living thing, seemingly affected by the tension that emanated from the team as we loaded our gear. The crew consisted of two local fishermen turned guides, one of whom busied himself around the boat, the other squeezing a substantial belly behind the steering wheel and flicking the engines into life.

As we headed into the open water, the phosphorescence around the boat left a comet's trail in our wake. The lights of the fishing fleet twinkled on the horizon, drawing ever closer as we surfed to-wards them, the sea coming alive at our passage to glow and pulse in our wake.

Reaching the first fishing vessel, the skipper stilled the engines, and we drifted gently alongside a multi-coloured dory with two swarthy fishermen hauling on long lines. As we arrived, one of the lines tightened, and with a grunt the fisherman began to haul it in hand over hand. Periodically he would stop as the creature on the end surged away into the darkness, before wordlessly re-commencing hauling and heaving. Abruptly there was a geyser of water and ink from beside the boat, like a grenade had been carelessly lobbed into the water. With a final grunt, he reached down and dragged a fiery red squid over the side, its body glistening in the moonlight, a nightmare glimpse of flailing tentacles and thrashing fins.

It was obvious that there were a great many squid beneath us, as each time the lures were dropped over the side of the fishing boat they were immediately seized, and battle would re-commence. Our guide nodded to the skipper, who put the engines into gear and moved the boat slowly to a point a couple of hundred meters away from the fishing boats. He dropped anchor, letting the line run through his hands for a seemingly interminable period, until it struck bottom.

It was at this point that we assumed the guide would kit up and lead us into the water. There was a moment's silence as we all looked at one another, the gear lying untouched between us. The guide looked baffled, before realization dawned. He muttered something in Spanish, which effortlessly bridged the language barrier by including a shrug and a puff on a cigarette that glowed in the darkness like a bright orange full stop. It seemed that for this dive at least we were on our own.

Simon, Jason and I lowered ourselves into the water, and slipped down the anchor line in a tight group. After some vigorous "After you" and "No, no, no, no, after you" exchanges, we finally settled at about a hundred feet. Huddling in the absolute blackness, pitch dark water beneath our trembling fin tips, we suddenly became aware of flashes of light beneath and around us. Big ones. Moving ones. Moving towards us ones.

I was then tapped roughly on the head from behind by what I thought was one of the cameramen. I looked up to see both of them several yards in front of me, looking at me with eyes the size of bantam eggs. A large squid was fondling my scalp, doubtless prior to removing a lump of it with furiously clicking beak. Fortunately it is in situations like this when ones experience and training immediately kicks in. In the finest traditions of the divers everywhere, I squealed like a piglet and span round, waving my

The fishermen haul out an extremely annoyed Humboldt squid. We look on wordlessly.

arms in a demented manner whilst calling in the most strident terms for my mum. This is an unusual reaction for the normal prey items of the squid, and it fled back to the Stygian gloom from whence it came.

Suddenly our tiny group was surrounded by squid, swooping in from the darkness from every direction. We span and twisted on the line, camera lights blazing as the alien forms of the squid pulsed and swirled around us. After that initial investigation, my heart was pounding and for a sickening moment I genuinely thought we had hugely miscalculated this encounter. The squid appeared in mobs, impossibly to track, and moving at such speed that we simply had no idea where they would come from next. We felt intensely vulnerable in the darkness, with no idea where the threat lay, and hopelessly ill-equipped to deal with it when it materialized.

It was then that a key aspect of the squid's behaviour appeared, one that would transform this encounter for us. In the darkness we could clearly see the squid surrounding us, closing in to investigate and hover. It was as we swung our lights on to them that they would immediately vanish back into the deep water, showing extraordinary acceleration for such a big animal.

These animals communicate by light, and to them our powerful camera lights and strobes must have represented nothing more than a monstrous squid. The lights were our protection, a haven that created a pool of safety in the blackness that surrounded us. Turn the lights off, and the pulsing bodies would close in, turn them on again and they would flee.

Gradually we relaxed, secure in the knowledge of our magical force field. Again and again the squid backed away from the lights, and we drove them before us as, emboldened, we moved away from the anchor line to hang in mid-water under the boat. The two guides had lowered glowing lures over the side, replicating the lantern fish that are a favoured prey of the squid. These were attacked furiously, on occasion several squid seizing a lure simultaneously to battle for possession. Our fear had been replaced by a real sense of wonder, surrounded as we were by pirouetting bodies pulsing with light and power. Simon and Jason tracked the squid in the gloom, flicking on their lights at the last moment to capture moments of predatory frenzy, whilst I gesticulated to camera, caught up entirely in the experience.

After half an hour of frantic activity, we surfaced to change cylinders and re-enter the fray. Within moments the squid found us again, arrowing out the darkness to attack the lures and investigate the strange figures that spun and gesticulated beside them. The squid grew bolder, taking the lures closer and closer to our lights, and even attempting the occasional brief fumble of a fin or arm in the gloom, jetting off the moment we turned out lights onto them. After another hour we had some tremendous shots, and returned once again to the surface.

Sitting on the boat, eyeing the remaining cylinders, we prepared to change our gear once again. We were all completely exhausted, functioning on adrenalin alone. Abruptly I caught Simon and Jason's eyes as they sat in the stern, and a look of complete understanding passed between us. Wordlessly we slipped the remaining cylinders back into the rack, and the skipper – picking up on the mood – reached forward to start the engines. The boat came to life, turning its nose towards the bright lights of the town in the distance, leaving the dark waters of the Sea of Cortez to the new masters of the night's hunt.

Opposite
The Humboldt squid doing what it does best, including a cannibalistic attack in images three and four.

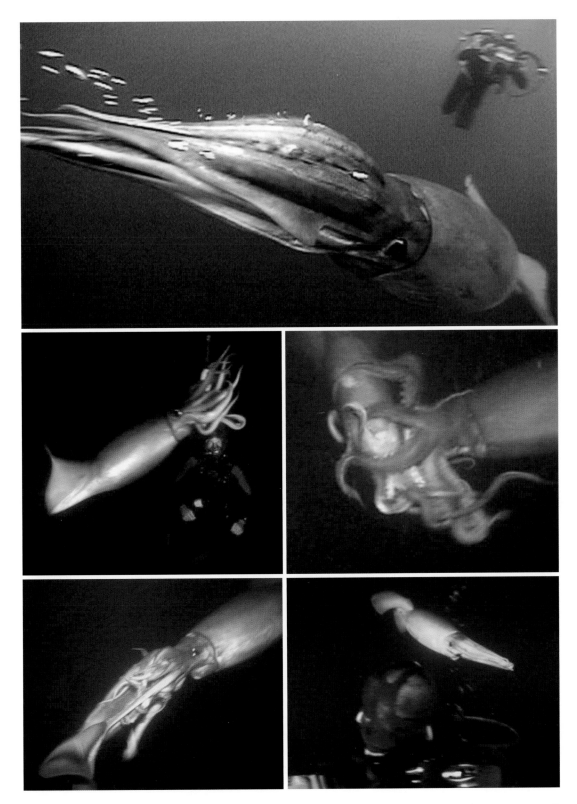

Chapter 4

The Monarch of the Sea

Canada and Norway

The Killer Whale

The Monarch of the Sea – The Killer Whale

Northern Vancouver Island on Canada's west coast is quite beautiful, absurdly green and lush, with pine forests plunging theatrically into ribbons of shining sea lochs. These in turn are criss-crossed by whales and sea otters, interspersed with the odd splash of a bald eagle spoiling a trout's afternoon. Flying over the network of rivers and inlets, it looked wild and untamed, a vision of wilderness perfectly in tune with the master predator that was our target animal.

Previous page
The northern lights over the Lefoton Islands, Northern Norway.

After landing at Vancouver Airport, we loaded a hire car to the point where the suspension squealed in protest and the wheels vanished into the arches, and set out on the road that runs up the east coast of the island. This is a sinuous tarmac track that follows the convoluted coastline, with the view of the channel mainly obscured by dense pine forests, which offer only brief glimpses of the achingly beautiful scenery beyond. Every gap in the trees was a

picture postcard, demanding much unloading and loading of camera kit accompanied by me driving slowly past in frame, an immensely tedious but essential process for the programme. Examine my face closely in the subsequent shots and you can faintly make out an expression that ranges from acceptance, to resignation, to tedium, and finally the glint of madness that you most certainly wouldn't want to glimpse in your rear view mirror on a lonely highway.

Having finally bagged the last travelling shots, we finished our journey to the northern tip of the island in darkness, checking into a clapperboard motel that sat in a lonely inlet, with whispering pine forest behind, and silent jet black water ahead. The next morning saw us wearily transferring our camera gear to the reassuringly stout boat of our host John de Brock for the final leg of our journey. John welcomed us on board with an easy smile and a handshake that enveloped my own hand in a mighty scarred paw. John was huge, a great ambling thing of a man. I very badly wanted him to be my friend, as the alternative was too awful to contemplate.

Sunset over Canada's Pacific coast

As we loaded the gear, John explained that the best way to get around in this neck of the woods is on the water. This is for two simple reasons – the first being that you see all manner of extraordinary activity as you putter through shaded inlets, and the second being that the roads run out just as you get to the really interesting bits.

We were with John to see killer whales, giant octopus, and – a personal ambition of mine – wolf eels. However, before heading off to the remote float home that acts as John's base, we had short detour to make.

The gloriously shambolic dive base.

We needed to film grizzlies fishing for salmon, and as we had neither the time nor the budget to launch a separate filming trip, we were joining a tourist excursion. John duly dropped us off at a nearby jetty where a group of particularly intrepid tourists were embarking on one of the day boats to get up close and personal with the grizzlies. This involves tracing a route up the nearby bays and inlets, ever watchful for a bear peering intently into the water. The bears – like any old angler – are notoriously grumpy when fishing, and the idea is to creep up on them as they concentrate on other things, trying to be as quiet as possible. The drawback is that this happens in an extremely large aluminium skiff. Try pushing a skip quietly down your local high street and you'll get an idea of how tricky this is.

After a search of several hours, we found a group of bears fishing in a small riffle off the main channel. Motordrives whirring and shutters snapping, we got really close to a bear that could only be described as substantial, and then abruptly the boat crunched on some gravel. The bear looked up and cogs plainly whirred in its "I eat absolutely anything" brain. Without wishing to read too much into its facial expression, it seemed to me that its thought processes went along the lines of "Why bother chasing salmon that swim like bullets when I can just wander over there and hoik out a fat American tourist and eat well for a week?" He duly ambled over, causing our guides to reverse our skiff, an emotional process as it is all done entirely by hand. The idea was to get to deep water, which we did as the bear was an exhilarating few metres away. This was accomplished by our guide pushing the boat out and then actually swimming in his waders, his little legs whirring frantically, whilst all we could see was a white set of knuckles on the side of boat. When I asked him later if that was normal, he looked at me with hollow eyes and, rather huskily, said "No."

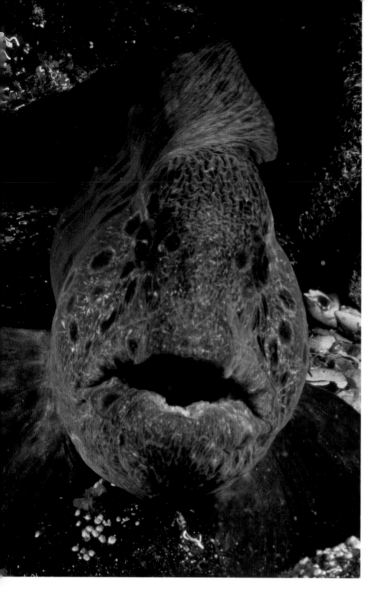

We were elated with our footage of a hungry bear a few feet from twenty trembling tourists in checked trousers, and returned to the jetty to find John waiting for us in the gathering gloom, ready for the very final leg of our journey to the backwater hideaway that was to be our home for the next week. This was an extraordinary place, essentially a log cabin floating on mighty timbers up a remote creek. John had furnished it from bits of flotsam and jetsam that had drifted in on the tide, the fixtures and fittings themselves speaking of distant shores and exotic seas.

We were up early the next morning for our dive with the wolf eels. These animals look remarkable, essentially an eight foot long blenny. They are – and there is only one way to say this – incredibly ugly, with a face that would make a funeral cortège turn

A wolf eel peers out of its lair. A face only a mother could love.

down a side street. As if appreciating that personality goes a long way, they are one of the friendliest of all fish, and seem to love divers. This is probably because they associate people with food (as divers have been feeding them for years), and also – bizarrely – like nothing more than having a dam good scratch.

We duly had a wonderful dive – really, really wonderful – with a huge wolf eel that gazed at me adoringly from about an inch away as I scratched it under the chin. The last time I was that close to something that ugly was an unfortunate lapse of judgement during a slow dance in Plymouth many years previously.

The giant octopus proved to be a tad more elusive. Nocturnal, rather shy creatures, they are only seen at night, and we went through a maddening period of a great deal of looking over a great many nights. Although this was frustrating in the extreme, it did give us a splendid chance to listen to John the Giant's stories as we waited for night to fall.

John had skippered a trawler for many years in the wild waters off Northern Canada, and knew a thing or two about big seas. He had

The team outside the float home, looking rather pleased with themselves after a splendid wolf eel dive.

also played rugby at the highest levels in Canada, and had what could only be described as a lived-in face, a lattice work of tiny scars, pits and lumps that told of dark deeds at the murky base of many a pile of heaving bodies. His hands were gnarled, sinewy plates, knotted by decades of hauling on icy ropes and the general attrition of keeping a working trawler afloat in the frigid waters to the far north.

For all of his gladiatorial past, John was a gentle, quietly spoken man, and had to be coaxed into telling stories of his life in the most dangerous profession of all. We would sit in the growing darkness of the wheelhouse as we waited for the final rays of the sun to die and night to settle over the rustling forest and silent inlets. When the wheelhouse was finally pitch black, with the only illumination the glowing end of John's cigarette, he would begin to talk in a basso rumble, a disembodied voice drifting out of the gloom to be absorbed by the wide eyed group of divers before him, like children around a camp fire.

Following a particularly lame story from me about a storm off Scotland, the highlight of which was a pile of plates falling off a shelf in the galley, I could see the end of the cigarette begin to smoulder volcanically, always the prelude to a particularly good story.

"Was in a big storm once myself." said John quietly. "I fought to keep the boat going through it, and then got hit by three freak waves. I slipped sideways down the face of the first, turned the boat on the top of the second, surfed straight down it and into the heart of the third."

Silence, punctuated only by the brief flare of an orange ember in the darkness.

"I was in the wheelhouse, sealed against the storm. The boat knifed straight into the base of the wave, and it went completely silent. All I could see was the green water outside the windows becoming darker as we went deeper. I braced myself against the windows, one hand on each, and it got quieter and darker still. A jet of water shot through the key hole of the cabin door, and went nine feet across the cabin to hit the instrument panel opposite."

"I felt the boat stop and settle, almost as though she was having a think about which way to go. The slowly she began to rise. The

John the Giant in his cabin, scene of many a great evening story.

wave had passed over us by now, and all the old girl had to do was get herself back to the surface. After a few moments it began to get light, and then we were back in the full fury of the storm again."

John had consulted an expert in hydrodynamics after the storm, and was told that given the diameter of the key hole, and the distance the water travelled through it, his small trawler must have been 65 to 70 ft underwater. A tiny capsule of air in the icy darkness, a lone man standing with his hands pressed against the windows of the wheelhouse, hurtling to what he thought was his death.

We sat in silence absorbing the story, our own tales of derring-do neatly put into perspective. The cigarette continued to glow quietly in the darkness.

After several fruitless nights searching every promising nook and cranny for the elusive giant octopus, John finally motored us many miles over water gilded by moonlight to where a craggy rock loomed through the water's surface – his absolute guaranteed octopus spot. The place looked like octopus heaven from the surface, and upon descending we were faced with a series of caves, overhangs and ledges, sprinkled with a promising collection of crab shells – shrapnel from an octopus buffet. Giant octopus are intensely curious animals, and we had been widely assured that if you wiggle your fingers (glove off) in front of the hole, the octopus will emerge. This I duly did, forgetting that the octopus is a distinctly bendy affair. After wiggling my hand in front of yet another dark cavern, I was somewhat perturbed when a tentacle emerged smartly from the hole to investigate my fingers. Six of the octopus's legs stayed glued to the inside of the den, and the remaining two wrapped themselves around my hand and dragged me in (well, my arm in – the rest of me stayed resolutely outside). We gurned at each other for about ten minutes from this position, both pulling in different directions and getting nowhere, until Jason got bored and hauled on the bits of me that remained outside the hole. The octopus emerged smartly, and a tremendous ten minutes ensued with him being filmed from all angles. Before we left, we guided him towards two fat crabs that had the misfortune to be ambling past, and left him munching on them contentedly.

Sadly, although we were enjoying some memorable wildlife encounters, the orcas remained elusive. The local grapevine was telling us in no uncertain terms that they were still many miles out to sea, and a hasty re-think was plainly required.

A series of phonecalls to an increasingly horrified accounts department at the tv company saw a magnificently ambitious plan take shape. We would re-pack our kit, and move the entire shoot across the world to northern Norway. When the plan was ultimately given the go ahead, there was an audible clunk at the other end of the phone line as the production manager – in charge of all matters financial – crumpled weakly into a creaking swivel chair.

It was therefore a distinctly poverty-stricken film crew that arrived at the Lofoton Islands in northern Norway several weeks later. Over a hundred miles north of the Arctic Circle, the islands are starkly beautiful, consisting of a Lord of the Rings-style landscape of dark mountains glazed with ice and snow, running the length of fjords that shimmered in the weak sunlight. The island chain is really more of a massive peninsula, with the settlement at the very tip called – with commendable brevity – A. This qualifies it as the shortest place name on earth, a record I'm not sure can ever be beaten. I am quietly convinced that A was named less after a local characteristic, and more after the noise the first explorer made as he stepped onto the blasted dark rock of the peninsula. I made a similar noise myself as I walked off the aircraft at Narvik Airport.

Travelling along the roads carved into the sides of the dark fjords towards our final destination of Henningsvar, it was impossible not to be struck by the stark beauty of this part of Norway. There is an all-pervading feeling that man does not quite belong here, and the fjords have such grandeur that they completely dominate the small settlements that cower in the steep sided bays or along the river mouths. The one thing the Norwegians have truly mastered is creating small havens of warmth and comfort in this magnificently unforgiving landscape, and we would often stop in gently lit cafes perched on the sides of the fjord to drink deliriously rich hot chocolate, hands cupped around steaming mugs, a fire crackling and spitting in the corner.

The magnificent icy mountains fringing the fjords of Northern Norway.

We arrived at the dockside in darkness, although this far north a milky sun only peers briefly over the horizon for a few hours anyway before sliding off behind the mountains that fringe the fjords. We skidded our way up the precipitous gangplank, cradling thousands of dollars worth of camera gear, wide-eyed and grabbing at icy guard rails. Awaiting us at the end of the gangplank was the good ship *MS Lamgoysund*, rocking gently at her mooring in the crisp night, lights glowing and generators rumbling.

The good ship MS Lamgoysund sits icily alongside the harbour.

The reason we were here was the presence of six hundred killer whales hunting in the dark waters of the fjord outside the harbour entrance. The killer whale is a creature that has fascinated mankind for as long as he has explored the sea. The Greek translation of *Orca* means 'killer from hell', a fair indication that orcas were not regarded with overwhelming affection by the early explorers. This is understandable, with the terrible spectacle of a pod of killer whales harassing and then killing a whale surely leaving an indelible impression on the earliest navigators.

We are now considerably wiser, and know that the orca is an intensely social animal, with the tightest of family bonds. Theirs is a matriarchal society, with each pod governed by females who will have given birth to all the males within the group. Females give birth only once every three years, and their male offspring never leave them, spending their entire lives – up to 60 years – in the company of their mothers. This is at the very heart of orca society, and tales abound of grief-stricken females carrying the body of a still-born baby orca in their mouths for many weeks. This is not altogether surprising given that females give birth only once every three years, and their offspring are bonded to them for life. Males adopt the classically dominant role in terms of defending the pod, and will frequently scout ahead looking for threats or a food source.

Orcas face the same problems as other cetaceans in that they store toxins in their blubber. This has served them splendidly for tens of thousands of years, until man began to belch waste and chemicals into the sea. The problem is compounded for the killer whales as they are at the very top of the food chain, with each animal they eat having in turn consumed its own share of pollutants. The buck stops with the orca. They are considered to be so polluted that when a dead killer whale is washed ashore, it is now officially classified as toxic waste.

The orcas in this part of Norway were chasing the great shoals of herring that aggregate in these waters. In the mid 1970s, the herring shoals had been decimated by over-fishing, falling from 14 million tonnes to a mere 50,000 tonnes. The remnants of these once mighty shoals sought refuge in the deep waters of the fjords, a final stand against the onslaught of man. Their more traditional enemy the orca followed them into the fjords, and the whale watching industry was born.

Initially, the orca paid a terrible price for this desperate pursuit of the herring into the domain of mankind. With mind boggling irony, the fishermen assumed that the appearance of more orca and the simultaneous disappearance of the herring were connected, and set about slaughtering the killer whales. Over 2,500 were destroyed, until protection was finally granted in 1981.

The fishermen and the orca now hunt herring in the same fjords, with the fishermen using purse seine nets, and the orca using a technique called carousel feeding. This is no easy matter, as the herring mass in water over a thousand feet deep, requiring a small number of the orcas to leave the main pod and dive into the pitch blackness below. They enter the gigantic main shoal, and using a series of buzzes, clicks and flashes of their white bellies, isolate a group of herring. Like huge sheepdogs they then have to herd the seething mass of herring to the surface. Once the herring have been bunched into a flailing, writhing ball, the orca move in one by one, beating the shoal with their tails, and eating the stunned fish. Although initially the complete herring is consumed, towards the end of the feeding spree, the orca will take only the best cuts of each fish, stripping away the flesh with remarkable dexterity in those terrible jaws. This behaviour is unique to orcas in Norway, although their unparalleled ability to adapt and learn has seen them successfully dominate the food chain wherever they appear in the ocean. A combination of speed, strength, guile, intelligence and the ability to hunt co-operatively means the orca is found in every ocean on earth, and they are the most widely distributed mammal in the world.

This extraordinary ability to adapt has seen the orca adopt the fishing boats as giant companions in their efforts to catch herring. Given the intense physical demands on orca of diving deep into the fjords, the orca have instead started to follow the boats, and sweep up any herring that escape the purse seine nets. Although the benefits to the fishermen are not known, and are probably non-existent, it seems the least man can do given his history with the orca in these troubled waters.

On entering the warm fug of the main saloon on board, it became immediately apparent that we were in the company of some very serious wildlife photographers indeed. Dark figures sporting several days of stubble crouched over mugs of coffee, big jumpers abounded, and there was a general air of serious endevour. There was a deathly hush as we moved our gear into the saloon, with the odd half smile, and at least one distinct glower from a chap whose face was illuminated only by the ghostly glow from his lap-top computer. The saloon was littered with gigantic lenses, and some extremely intrepid looking cold weather gear hung behind the door. This was no place for the faint hearted, and I felt slightly ridiculous in my woolly hat and a scarf I had borrowed from my big sister. We had also, with touching naivety, bought along our wetsuits, and my disquiet turned into considerable alarm as I looked at the black vulcanized monsters of drysuits hanging in the dry store.

The reason for all of this gear became horribly apparent the next morning, as the sun clambered up the side of the fjord and perched wearily just above the lip of the stark mountain range that guarded it. The wind whistled outside, lifting the edges of portholes and hatches, trying to get at the warmth within with shrieking tendrils, howling in frustration. Our guide advised us to wrap up warmly

– although I had no idea at the time of the yawning gulf between "wrapping up warmly" in Bristol, and the equivalent in Norway.

We were to spend the next five hours – the entire duration of the daylight hours – bouncing around the fjord in an open boat looking for orcas. We were soon nosing out of the harbour and into an exquisite sunrise that made the snow and granite mountains opposite glow in stark contrast against the dark water below. The only thing detracting from the grandeur of the spectacle was the fact that Jason had forgotten his warm hat, and had had to borrow one from Karen. He stood on the deck, draped in lenses and hardcore cold weather gear, sporting a fluffy lady's hat that had two furry bobbles on the very top. He looked like a man balancing a pair of polar bear testicles on his head, and became increasingly tight lipped at the muffled titters that followed his progress around the boat.

Heading out into the fjord in the teeth of an icy wind.

Our guide Asgeir spotted his growing chagrin, and leant over with some words of wisdom forged in many an icy Norwegian winter:

"My friend, out here it's not how you look, it's how you feel."

These words proved prophetic, and within moments of turning into the teeth of the wind, my entire face had gone numb. Offered some coffee, I dribbled it around flaccid lips, cup clasped in one claw-like hand. Looking for the orcas demanded that all of us peer through weeping slitty eyes into the middle distance, all the while gurning and gasping. The boat resembled some sort of special outing, and it was no surprise that the orcas gave us a wide berth. Glancing down at the dark water, the wind whipping icy crests into a stinging shrapnel of freezing spray, the idea of lowering myself into it seemed so utterly monstrous that I quietly hoped the orcas would remain out of sight.

Monty shows his great pleasure at the prospect of a day out on the water.

Such hopes were dashed with a shout from Asgeir, and following his outstretched arm I clearly made out the drifting mist of a spout from an orca, then another and seconds later another. The boat's engine, for most of the day gently idling behind us, came to life, and raised its tempo to a resolute bellow, driving us through the water towards the distant pod.

About a hundred metres away from the first sighting the skipper slowed the boat, and once again idled slowly forward, all of us scanning the waters ahead silently. I was staring directly at a patch of water off our bow, thrashing and writhing in the wind, when in the midst of it a small shape appeared. This gradually grew in size, like the conning tower of a submarine knifing through the surface, until revealing itself in all its glory as the six foot dorsal fin of a male orca. As the lead male arched a great dark back, marked with the distinct white saddle-like markings, two smaller fins broke the surface further behind.

There is evidence emerging that the male orcas, in their traditional role as the protectors of the main pod, are drawing the whale watching boats away from their family groups. It appears that the males will slowly swim on the surface, loitering close to the boats and leading them slowly into the fjord as the more vulnerable families move discreetly into the fishing grounds in the background. This is only speculation at present, although the three whales ahead of us certainly seemed in no hurry to move away from the noisome buzzing of the boat.

After circling the orcas for several minutes – or perhaps they were circling us – the skipper gave the word that we should prepare to jump in. This raised a range of emotions that plunged me into inner turmoil. There was the obvious disinclination to lower my skinny frame into freezing Arctic waters, but over-riding all other sensations was the primeval instinct not to jump into a small patch of water in front of three huge orcas who were plainly here to hunt.

I slipped over the side of the boat, barely noticing the icy water creeping down the back of my neck and into my suit. The moment of truth came as I pushed reluctantly away from the side of the boat to float face down in the fjord, the final gesture where I became committed to the encounter and put my trust entirely in the killer whales around me.

I lay still for what seemed an age on the surface, my legs feeling intensely vulnerable as they dangled enticingly in the water behind me. Visibility was excellent, around thirty feet or so, and gave the water an eerie green glow. I was suspended above the world of the orca, hovering in space, watching a three-dimensional stage below me for an appearance of three great black and white bodies.

Having peered downwards for several minutes, and feeling the first chill creep into my bones as if my body was awakening from the torpor of the ancient survival instincts roused by the early moments of the encounter, I lifted my head to look at the boat. As I did so, Asgeir gestured frantically to the water behind me, and turning to look, there was the majestic fleet of fins, perhaps a hundred feet away, slowly arcing down on a shallow dive. They were heading directly towards me, and with the boat fifty or so metres away, I was entirely isolated in their path.

I lowered my face back into the fjord, fear replaced by curiosity and an overwhelming desire to glimpse an orca in the wild at last. The green water ahead of me remained impassive, weak sunlight shimmering and dancing in the shallows, and then, on the absolute limit of my vision, appeared a killer whale.

The orca was barely moving, gently sculling towards me presenting a face-on view of that great dark orb of a body. There was an unmistakable impression of power, an animal in complete control of its element, unchallenged master of its domain. Sculling ever closer, the angle between us narrowed until I was presented with a glimpse of the orca's flank, the first flash of white markings almost iridescent in the water. At the zenith of the encounter the gap between us narrowed to twenty feet. As the orca swept by 20ft beneath me, it turned to peer inquisitively at this strange creature above.

Even with all that power and grace on display, the beauty of the markings, the majestic promise of subdued power, and the grandeur of the setting, there is only one thing that commands attention when confronted by an orca in the wild. It is the eye. As the orca swept beneath me, the eye tracked me, intelligence and curiosity reflected in his gaze. This is an animal we have feared, hunted and harried, as well as diminishing its major food source beyond measure. It is only in the last generation that we have started to

The unmistakable dorsal fin of a male orca.

appreciate the orca as the most magnificent co-operative hunter in the sea, an intelligent socially aware mammal perhaps closer to us than we care to realise. As I turned in the water to follow the orca beneath me, I wondered what questions stirred in that great brain. The whale disappeared into the fjord to continue its journey, the sound of its family resonating in the water, a peculiar piece of flotsam floating behind it, staring dumbstruck at the monarch of the sea.

Two male orcas spy hopping at the approach of the whale watching boats.

Chapter 5

The Grey Juggernaut

Scotland

The Basking Shark

The Grey Juggernaut – The Basking Shark

The small town of Tobermory presents an idyllic image of a Scottish fishing community. Rows of brightly coloured houses line a harbour full of painted trawlers, with seagulls squabbling over scraps on the quay, the whole scene set against dark hills covered in heather.

There was a slightly different feel to our week of filming this time. For a start we were in Scotland, which delighted me as I had always wanted to include a British destination in the Great Ocean Adventure series. As an added treat the film crew consisted entirely of my friends, selected not only for their diving skills, but also their considerable social potential. One doesn't head into the very heart of a set of islands famed for their whisky production without a hand-picked team! Simon and Jason from Scubazoo had taken a well deserved break after their heroics of the last few weeks, and around me were an eclectic mix of relatives (Russ, my brother-in-law and an ex-commercial diver), ex-military types (Chris, a bomb

Previous page
Preparing for departure on the jetty, attempting to ignore the storm in the background.

104

disposal diver the size of a well-fed bison), and hardy underwater cameramen (Dan Burton and Dan Stevenson). All these occupations require masochistic tendancies as the diving conditions of British waters are among the most demanding on earth.

This disparate group shared a vast range of experience, plus the powerful unifying factor of consistently finding the act of breaking wind amusing. Our tranquil passage through the Western Isles, for so many years an inspiration for scholars, poets and writers, was therefore punctuated by peculiar parping noises followed immediately by roars of mirth and mutual congratulation.

We were all old friends, and as such when the group drove down into Tobermory the discussion in the mini-bus resembled less that of a serious camera crew and more of a well-oiled stag night. The week would represent a chance to sample local whiskies, tell tall stories, and generally catch up on several years of gossip. And if there's one thing I've learned about British divers, it's that they like a good gossip, nattering away like old fishwives at the first opportunity.

Tobermory harbour in a rare moment of clear weather during our visit.

Monty tells a story. Chris and Dan look politely interested.

Of course there was also a large animal in the equation. This was no whimsical, pseudo giant we had managed to squeeze into the series to ensure we had a British destination. It was a genuinely mammoth animal, in fact the second largest fish in any ocean, and one that science still knows very little about. We were in Tobermory to film the basking shark.

Having done a quick inspection of the harbour and town, we drove back up the hill to our tiny Bed and Breakfast. Pleasingly, this was once again precisely how you'd imagine a B&B in somewhere called Tobermory to be – picturesque in the extreme, with the occasional stag peering through the flowerbeds, and run by a landlady who was 4'10' tall. I know that because she rather proudly told me when we met, although initially I had no idea where the voice was coming from and peered about me wildly before looking down and spotting her.

The arrival of several large men with even larger bags created an instant scene of utter bedlam. I left as one of the more absurd bags was being manoeuvred with a great deal of shouting through a corridor, and wandered back down the hill to meet up with our skipper for the week.

About an hour later I was sitting with the small figure of Paul, proud skipper of *The Silver Swift*. It was already a day when we seemed to have wandered onto the film set of *Whisky Galore*, and Paul was undoubtedly the best character so far. He oozed the wisdom of the Western Isles, rasping a weathered thumb over grey beard as he peered at our ludicrous list of target species. Finally, he glanced up and peered at me over the top of half-moon specs.

"You don't want much do ya laddie? I should tell you that we've just had the Discovery Channel up here for three weeks, and they got bugger all in terms of basking shark images. I'll do my best of course, but I can't promise anything."

Seeing my crestfallen look, he smiled and patted me on the shoulder, "Don't worry laddie, they're out there somewhere. And if they're there, I'll find 'em for you."

With that, he turned and departed for his boat, leaving behind him only a thoughtful silence and the faintest whiff of kelp.

Before our search for the basking sharks could begin, there were two other compelling draws to the waters beyond the harbour entrance. One was a wreck that had a certain level of fame amongst divers in the UK, and the other was the darker side of man's relationship with the basking shark.

First off was the wreck dive, our introduction to the cold waters around the Isle of Mull, and a chance to check out our gear and systems before encountering the basking sharks in the open water. The next morning we loaded *The Silver Swift*, a small, neat boat that reflected its skipper precisely. Motoring out to the site, we were in the finest of fine moods. It was a beautiful day, with the loch's surface shimmering gently in the autumnal sunlight. Cormorants sunned themselves on the rocks as we passed, spreading dark wings and peering at us with wary eyes. The pine forests on the edge of the loch parted occasionally to offer tantalizing glimpses of grand feudal castles. There was a delicious familiarity to puttering across UK waters once again, where I had served my shivering diving apprenticeship in many a silty tidal race off the south coast of England. A steaming mug of tea was handed wordlessly out of the cabin by Paul, and for the moment at least, my life was complete.

Diving a wreck can be a wonderfully melancholy experience, as they provide the most atmospheric backdrop to the story of their sinking, frozen for a moment in time when the winds howled and the waves crashed. One of the real fascinations of wrecks is the story behind them, and this wreck – like all wrecks – hid a tale of drama, and in this case, of heroism.

She was a Swedish merchant vessel called the *Hispañia*, and the skipper had chosen to go down with her. This was in 1954 mind you, and he had plenty of opportunities to be rescued, but steadfastly to leave his ship. It sends a distinct shiver down the spine to drift through the wheelhouse and imagine him gripping the wheel as the stricken vessel shuddered and settled beneath him.

The thing that makes the *Hispañia* special is the marine life. It sits in the heart of a tidal race on the loch floor, and is the equivalent of an underwater apartment block, dropping mysteriously from the surface and providing numerous dark hideaways and flat surfaces for colonization. The wreck had quickly become a city under the sea, with dodgy neighborhoods where (if you were a shrimp) you most certainly wouldn't want to be caught out after dark.

The dive itself was wonderful, with slate grey conger eels peering at me from dark pipes, and silver pollack patrolling overhead like squadrons of aircraft. On the surface of the wreck itself, prehistoric,

Ballan wrasse in its multi-coloured livery.

brightly coloured tub gurnard lurked, whilst wolf fish stared from dark hatches, looking like trolls in a cave.

As I ascended I reflected that diving in the UK really could match anything on earth, and an expression of considerable satisfaction settled on my face as I hung on the anchor line. This was sharply replaced with an expression of some alarm as one of my ankle seals on my suit split, resulting in a flood of icy loch water creeping up my inner thigh. This was not a sensation I would recommend, and saw me exiting the water with an athleticism that surprised everyone, springing onto the boat vertically like a penguin onto an ice flow.

The next day we woke to hissing rain, making diving tricky, and filming impossible. Scotland is famous for both its whisky and it's golf, and having already sampled the whisky with some enthusiasm, it seemed as good an opportunity as any to introduce Chris to the great game. I took him to a course that was so beautiful it made me want to burst into song, and gave him a brief and intensely patronizing introduction to golf. I should point out at this juncture that my golf experience is considerable, whilst Chris's is nil. As in he'd never, ever, picked up a club. After he had patiently listened to my introductory lesson, we tee'd off, the loch glimmering below, and the wet heather shining around us as a weak sun peeked through a gap in the clouds.

Fast forward to the ninth hole. Chris is now striding the undulating course, head up, swinging a golf club as an impromptu walking stick, inhaling glorious Scottish air extravagantly through his nostrils and telling me this was quite the finest afternoon he's had for months. I am trailing several yards behind him, muttering darkly to myself, hands in pockets and kicking stones. Quite unreasonably, he has in

A lobster in a dark nook in the *Hispania*.

the interim cracked a series of 250 yard arrow-straight drives down various fairways, and is thrashing me. Each of his glorious shots is greeted by a truculent mumble from the surly git I've become, and a beaming smile from him. We ended up on the final green with me staring at my shoes, shaking his outstretched hand in much the same way a man would respond to being handed a turd.

Thankfully the weather improved and our filming could re-commence. The second pilgrimage was to the tiny island of Soay. It was here in 1948 that Gavin Maxwell, the author of the magnificent *Ring of Bright Water*, set up Scotland's first basking shark processing fishery. The story of this epic undertaking – *Harpoon at a Venture* – is an unparalleled tale of hardship, misfortune, and resolve. I was very keen indeed to briefly visit the island and pay my respects.

The island itself was tiny, and completed deserted. The ruins of the basking shark processing plant – in reality nothing more than a small cottage surrounded by incongruously massive machinery – stood silent under leaden skies. The site had been abandoned in the sixties, and is slowly giving itself up to the heather, seaweed, and small, scuttling inhabitants of the island.

The most striking aspect of the plant was the machinery, great rusting hulks of furnaces, winches, pulleys and rendering plants. The overwhelming impression was of immense industrial might, and as I peered into the cavernous maw of one of the main furnaces, any doubts that our target animal was anything other than a genuine giant were dispelled.

The basking shark is vast by any set of parameters. It weighs the same as three African elephants, with the adults tipping the scales at about seven tons. The largest measure about 35 ft from nose to tail, although there were well-substantiated rumours of a 40ft bruiser cruising the waters around Mull shortly before we arrived. This massive form guides itself through the water with the tiniest of on-board computers – even basking shark enthusiasts couldn't claim that these animals are intellectuals. The brain of a basking shark is about the same size as a rat's. Their intellectual capacity is summed up in a couple of lines penned many years before by poet Norman McCaig, agog at the monster before him:

"... I once met, on a sea tin-tacked with rain
that room-sized monster with a matchbox brain."

The basking shark has dispensed with a large brain quite simply because it has no need for one. The business end of the shark consists of a cavernous mouth, about a metre across in the largest sharks. When feeding, the mouth gapes, revealing white gill rakers that almost encircle the shark's head. The white colour is thought to be an attractant for light-sensitive plankton, which are swept into the mouth as the shark powers through the seas. They are guided by an extraordinarily sensitive nose, packed with sensory organs that guide them towards plankton aggregations, like a gently drifting deep-sea stealth bomber. Operating on a high intellectual plane just isn't required – swim, follow nose, open mouth, eat, grow, meet Mrs Basking shark, mate, die. Hardly astro-physics.

The great mystery used to be where these sharks went in the winter months, with legends of them hibernating on the muddy seafloor adding to the general confusion and mild hysteria as to their whereabouts. Recent research has indicated that the sharks stay pretty much in the same waters throughout the year, feeding constantly and diving up to a kilometre into the deep ocean to find plankton. The nose and the gills are one of the last parts of the basking shark to decompose when the animal washes ashore, leading to numerous reports of sea monsters as incredulous Victorians found massive, foul-smelling corpses that looked precisely like a child's idea of a dinosaur.

Our particular basking shark hunt finally got underway in earnest the next morning, and a slate grey dawn saw us all scanning a horizon optimistically as the boat weaved its way around the islands. We were, however, facing a fundamental problem. Although this is a massive animal, only the very tip of the dorsal fin shows at the surface. With a chop on the sea of a couple of feet, every shadow was a fin, and every distant puffin sighted led to excited shouts from the team. The assembled divers stuck to the job manfully, squinting through slitted eyes into the Scottish rain as it hissed into a bleak and choppy sea.

Soon the rain was the classic horizontal Scottish variety, and it seemed to me that every living thing was cowering in whatever passed as home. Only idiots like us were out in the teeth of the squall, and hope was waning as any basking shark would be deep in the gloomy water beneath us. Voicing my fears to Chris, he looked at me witheringly and said something splendid.

"Monty, I reject your reality of not seeing a basking shark, and I insert my own. At precisely 12:30 we will see our first shark." Turning smartly on his heel, he returned to his post, rain dripping from a granite chin thrust defiantly into the sheets of rain. If the boat had sunk he would still be there, grimly scanning the horizon whilst standing to attention as he slipped beneath the waves.

Indomitable Royal Engineer Chris Holt at his post.

Despite Chris's commendable resolve, things were looking bleak. Every local we had spoken to in the last week had informed us that it had been an appalling season for basking sharks, and a few days optimistically puttering around the island simply wasn't going to be enough. The addition of steadily worsening weather added to our woes.

And then something extraordinary happened. In complete contradiction to the incumbent weather conditions, the sun burst from behind a cloud, and the water miraculously stilled. Russ squinted into the middle distance, and idly muttered "What's that?" whilst pointing at two tiny triangles moving through the water's surface. And then, miraculously, we were surrounded by basking sharks. Everyone on the boat stood with their mouths open, remnants of the rain steaming off waterproofs, pointing in ten different directions. I glanced at my watch – it was 12:30. I looked across at Chris, who raised a single eyebrow and knowingly tapped the side of his nose. There are obviously some strange things going on in Royal Engineers training nowadays.

It took some time for the sharks to become accustomed to our presence, and there was a tense period where it looked as though they would be too skittish to allow us to enter the water alongside them. In our favour we were sitting in the midst of what was plainly a massive plankton aggregation, with the water the colour of pea soup and swarms of jellyfish drifting past the boat. Every time the sharks sounded, they would appear again moments later, mouths agape to sweep up countless millions of the microscopic life around them.

The moment finally came when we were cruising alongside one of the sharks, and Paul gave a quick nod as he cut the engines. This was our signal to enter the water, and I slipped into the green water swiftly followed by the two Dans.

It's actually pretty intimidating approaching basking sharks, as one is fighting a fundamental instinct. Generally, when floating on the water's surface as a large fin approaches, the standard reaction is, of course, to flee with some enthusiasm to any nearby boat.

We hung together on the water's surface, the shark sculling that great tail and moving towards us. The dorsal fin was only a few metres away when it suddenly submerged, and as one we lowered our faces into the water. The visibility was appalling, and yet there was no mistaking the great dark shape moving directly towards us.

Basking sharks make the most of a dense plankton bloom.

As it approached we gave a kick of our fins and allowed it to pass between us. The tiny eye regarded us with what seemed like only passing interest, and then the vast dappled flank, like the side of a tanker, passed before us endlessly until finally came the great sickle of the tail. A first encounter that we could only have dreamed of.

Basking sharks are of course filter feeders, but to see one pass beneath your twitching fins like a submarine still awakens some fairly primeval urges. It took a little time before I truly relaxed with the shark, and indeed for the shark became accustomed to our presence. Several more passes showed that the animal was

One of the team dwarfed by a feeding basking shark.

Opposite
The awesome spectacle of an approaching basking shark in feeding mode.

becoming more and more relaxed, until a pass took place with that massive mouth agape, appearing out of the gloom like a white cavern. This was the ultimate sign that the shark was accustomed to the presence of the divers, and the two Dans went into overdrive, filming this majestic animal from all angles as it swept past again and again. I simply hung in the water, turning slowly on my axis as I shared a patch of water with one of nature's giants off the magical Scottish isles.

Chapter 6

The Wandering Minstrel

Tonga

The Humpback Whale

The Wandering Minstrel –
The Humpback Whale

We arrived in the tiny island group of Va Va'u in northern Tonga in a rattly old Dakota. This was very much an Indiana Jones "having a fight whilst entangled in a cargo net hanging out the back door" style plane, and the islands passed beneath me in a blur while I was being shaken until my teeth chattered by engines that hadn't had a good service since the Berlin airlift.

As we flew in on arrival, I glanced down and saw two things. The first was a humpback whale, rolling in the surf at the end of the runway, the second (and, in a tragic reflection of my set of priorities, just as significant a sight) was several games of rugby going on in the fields around the airport. Ever since being lobbed a rugby ball at the tender age of seven, I have had a passion for the game that goes well beyond the obsessive. Sadly a large, and quite possibly yellow, streak of self preservation meant that I could never make the

Previous page
The sleepy port at
Va Va'u.

122

jump from enthusiastic amateur to snarling pro in my playing days, but nonetheless I take the chance to watch, think about, and even organize rugby matches whenever and wherever I travel. The last attempt had been a game of touch rugby with a bewildered group of fishermen in Indonesia, none of whom spoke English, but pretty much all of whom did me for pace at one point or another during the game. I was delighted to be landing in Tonga, as the rugby players of these islands are famed throughout the world, a splendid distraction for me from the main event of our target animal.

We were here to swim alongside a genuine ocean giant, as Tonga is the only place on earth where snorkelling with humpback whales is permitted. The humpback is a truly vast animal, over 15m (50ft) long and weighing 40 tonnes. From time immemorial humpbacks have travelled in great circles in the ocean, both in the northern and southern hemispheres – the two separate groups of animals never meeting. They move between their feeding grounds and their breeding grounds, the Tonga humpbacks visiting the cold rich waters of the Antarctic to stock up on krill, then migrating to

Sunset off the Tongan islands and another day searching for the whales ends.

123

the warm waters of Tonga to give birth and raise their young. This round trip of 10,000km is thought to be the longest migration of any mammal, a voyage that spans oceans, climates and time zones. The waters around Tonga are clear, calm and warm – the ideal place to nurse the young calves that lack the insulation of thick blubber required to survive in the colder feeding grounds. The mothers will not feed during this period, losing up to a quarter of their body weight before racing south again, their calves finally large enough to brave thousands of miles of big seas and cold waters. During nursing, the calves will take on 50 gallons of milk a day, 40% of which is pure fat, causing the calves to gain a kilogramme of weight every hour during feeding.

Although the numerous craggy bays and inlets that make up the 169 islands of Tonga provide many secluded spots for the whales, there are hazards for them even here. Huge tiger sharks follow the pregnant female whales, hoping to dine off the afterbirth, but also not averse to taking a calf at the moment of birth if the mother drops her guard. This is when the whales are at their most vulnerable, with many hungry mouths in the ocean around mother and calf ready to take advantage of a new-born animal that measures fifteen feet from nose to tail, and weighs a ton.

Perversely, as we arrived at this land of giants, the first thing we had to do was collect our bags from the smallest baggage carousel in the tiniest arrivals building I had ever seen. Having done so, we moved out into the warmth of a Tongan afternoon to hail a cab. As an ancient taxi drew up, the driver got out and approached one of the more ridiculously gigantic bags, weighing in at about 30 kgs or so. "Careful with that one" I said, "it's pretty heavy." He gave me a look of genuine bewilderment as he picked it up and flicked it into the back of the cab.

Rugby's a good game for the Tongans. There are many ways to describe them, but perhaps a simple "massive" is one of the best. This is where rugby legend Jonah Lomu comes from, and he only left because the big boys kept nicking his dinner money and giving him wedgies in the playground. Fortunately for the rest of the world, another word is "friendly". I like to think that I'm a large-ish chap (6'3" and about fifteen stone) but in the space of one short flight from Auckland to Tonga, I went from being a big bloke to being a skinny anaemic runt.

As our driver climbed into the taxi, I suddenly had a vivid mental image of an elephant trying to get into a fridge. The suspension of the cab groaned, and he grasped the steering wheel delicately between two fingers and thumbs, peering through the windscreen out of one eye, his head at an angle against the roof and one buttock-sized cheek pressed up against the glass. Tonga is one of the few nations on earth never have to been colonized by a western power, and although some put this down to the lack of natural resources on the islands making them unworthy of exploration, the fact that they are populated by huge, proud people with a fierce warrior heritage may have also had something to do with it. Despite their gentle day to day demeanour, Tongan warriors have been feared throughout the ages. They colonized much of eastern Fiji, and it was believed that they had magical powers which transformed them into sharks so they could travel the vast distances between the islands. These legends actually arose from their superb sea-faring skills, allowing them to conquer a great triangle of the Pacific that they referred to as "many islands", or "Polynesia".

We drove at breakneck speed through single lane roads shaded by palms into the small harbour that is the gateway to Va va'u, and received a warm welcome from the (relatively) Lilliputian figure of

Al, the owner of our host centre Dolphin Divers. Al is an ex-fireman from Wolverhampton, and when I asked him if he missed home he replied "No Monty, not at all." Substitute the word "Monty" in that sentence with "you blithering idiot" and you can probably get an idea of his facial expression at the time. And he had a point. Tonga is wild, untamed, full of the nicest people you could ever hope to meet, and remains relatively unsullied by tourists. Al soon had our gear stowed in the boat ready for our departure the next morning, and sat back on the dock as the sun began to set, cup of coffee in his hand as he explained the routine for seeking out the humpbacks.

The Tongan tribe of humpbacks is one of the smallest of the many that visit the Pacific islands in the summer months, and as yet not a great deal is known about them. There are thought to be about 300 whales that are regular visitors, however this number may vary slightly from year to year. The whale watching industry in Tonga is still relatively young, and as with any adolescent, is struggling to come to terms with rules and regulations. There is supposed to be a strict "one boat for one whale" rule, however this is frequently flaunted, and whales may be harried by several boats for several hours. This is particularly distressing for mothers with calves, and efforts are being made to curb the excesses of the more enthusiastic operators.

"The whales come here to rest, because they see it as a safe haven" said Al. "It's our responsibility to see that it stays that way. They are our honoured guests in these waters, and we should be responsible hosts."

There are more ominous developments afoot for the whales, with the Japanese putting pressure on the impoverished Tongan government to renew whaling in their waters. This would be a massacre, a hideous bloodbath as the whales swam into a confined ambush, and an event that would create a scar on the Tongan people in the eyes of the outside world that would never heal.

There is also hope however, for the whale watching industry brings in approximately 5 million dollars per year, revenue that increases annually. The people of Tonga love their reefs and wildlife, being the first of the Pacific nations to set up marine reserves. Above all they revere the whales, and as such are fiercely proud and protective of them. Should the government allow the whaling boats to move in, I feel sure they would be met by the re-kindled warrior spirit that once made the Tongans so feared. Perhaps the massacre would take place, but the price would be a dear one even for the industrial might of the Japanese whalers.

"If we see a whale," said Al, "we'll hang off it and see if it chooses to come over and have a look at us. They can be extremely curious and playful, and if we get the right animal you'll have an experience that you will never, ever forget. Patience is the name of the game. We go to the more remote islands, we motor along gently, and we wait – simple as that."

Next morning, bright and early, we were stood on the dock desperate to encounter our first humpback in the wilds of the open ocean – surely one of the ultimate wildlife encounters on the planet. Al turned up a few moments later, smiling at our obvious excitement. Trotting at his heels was Hobbs, his collie dog – who, Al informed us with only slight twinkle in his eye, had a near mythical ability to sense whales nearby. After piling aboard, and steaming into the channel amidst the normal bedlam one associates with a busy dive boat, we nosed past the main island, and soon were

Al keeps a watchful
eye alongside faithful
whale hound Hobbs.

bobbing about in the middle of nowhere, getting sunburnt noses
and squinting at the horizon optimistically. The islands offered a
stunning theatrical backdrop to our slow progress, their volcanic
origins apparent in plunging razor sharp ridges and echoing sea
caves. Tonga experiences the fastest plate movement of any set of

Opposite
Tonga is full of
echoing, mysterious
underwater caves.

Simon and Monty in position. Five days later we weren't looking quite so chirpy.

islands in the world, crunching and grinding along at a geological blur of 10cm a year, and is heading inexorably towards Samoa. What will happen when the (independent and warlike) islands of Tonga finally crunch into the (independent and warlike) islands of Samoa doesn't bear too much close thought. Happily the ensuing mother of all punch ups between the island's inhabitants will be witnessed only by future generations, and I shall be long gone.

Simon and I sat on the rear step of the boat, feet dangling in the water. We scanned the sea, getting burnt to a cinder, frying our corneas, and generally becoming pink, sweaty and irritable. The perception of wildlife filming is one of endless glamour, however there are inordinate hours of searching an empty sea, the gentle rising throb of a headache making its presence felt, every shadow and breaking wave a potential animal.

The few whales we did see were on the move, and were plainly not interested in us or the boat. The few times we slipped into the water, the whales would dive beneath us, allowing us only a tantalizing glimpse of disappearing white pectoral fins, 15 ft long and glowing eerily as they passed into the distance. Humpbacks can dive for up to forty five minutes, and cover huge distances during that period, so all we could do was stare forlornly after them. It was also not hugely advisable to hang around for too long on the surface, as the sinister entourage of tiger sharks that may or may not be lurking in the gloom could well take an interest in your floating, splashing form. At least one guide has been bitten in the past, and only a few months before a young girl had been taken in the shallows as she took an ill-advised late night swim.

The shadows finally lengthened, and Al moved to the back of the boat and patted us each on the shoulder. It was time to head for home, and after landing we wearily climbed the hill to our hotel, to sleep and dream of great blue forms twisting in the darkness.

The next day presented an opportunity to film on land around the islands, and also for me to set off in pursuit of a game of rugby. I had spent much of the previous day whipping our Tongan dive guide Ali into a frenzy about how I was going kick his steely butt on the rugby pitch at some point during our stay. This was, of course, complete nonsense, matching an occasional Old Bristolian 2nd XV wheezy winger (when selected) against 300lb of snorting fast twitch muscle with a warrior heritage and tattoos created with a sharpened pig bone. The sensation of being picked up and driven face first into concrete hard earth, with the rest of my body being crammed accordion-like into my skull, would probably have been moderately unpleasant but no more than I deserved.

Judicious juggling of the itinerary during our one land-based day meant that the game never took place. As I prepared to return to hotel at the end of the day, I bumped into Ali in the bustling streets of the harbour, and mentioned how he had got lucky that I hadn't had a chance to give him a good going over on the pitch. As such, the final sound I heard as I walked up the hill was his hysterical mirth, a fitting sound to finish the day in these islands where the default setting seems to be the smile.

The next morning found us again perched on the step at the back of the boat, lulled into a stupor by the heat, the gentle thump of the diesel engine, and the rocking of the boat in the oily swells. Still scanning the horizon, in the distance I suddenly saw a massive form break through the surface, falling back in an explosion of spray. Ali immediately turned the boat towards the horizon. The beat of the engine became more strident, and moments later we were in the midst of a scene of primal fury.

The whales do not come to Tonga only for rest and peace. Young males will vie for the attention of females, singing echoing, haunting melodies that carry for over 20km and are extremely complex, the love song of a forty ton animal. Should a female appear accompanied by other males, battle will commence. We had motored into the midst of what is termed a "heat run", essentially a fight for supremacy between ocean-going juggernauts.

The scene was dramatic enough from the surface, with explosions of spray and foam marking the collisions between the whales. Using

those massive pectoral fins, no longer elegant sails but brutal clubs, the whales beat and thrashed one another, occasionally breaking through the tumultuous surface to lunge at a rival, forcing him under through sheer body weight. What it must have looked like beneath the surface defied imagination.

The aftermath of the heat run. Foam and fury like exploding depth charges.

133

We were profoundly affected on the boat, the whiff of testosterone and fury of the encounter perhaps passed straight onto us as males of our own species. The tectonic scale of the impacts took our breath away. Entering the water was out of the question, as a lethal tonnage of charging whale could sweep aside and crush tiny, brittle boned creatures such as ourselves. I turned to the dive team to make my feelings known, only for a swift head count to note that we were one down.

I spun round to stare wide-eyed into the middle of the mêlée, and there was the minute form of Simon, legs pumping, snorkel waggling, and camera whirring. Around him were explosions of spray and building-sized shadows racing through the blue, and yet he was in his element. He returned to the boat a few minutes later, grinning broadly. It was two elemental forces of nature coming together in the midst of the ocean: Simon the demented underwater cameraman in the midst of a pack of hormonally charged whales.

Although this was a tremendous spectacle, it was not an encounter we could safely film, so we left the whales in the midst of their fury and continued to motor around the islands, scanning the bays and calm water around us. This scene was repeated through the next five days, with a steadily increasing sense of desperation pervading the boat. We had always been a lucky film crew, and yet each day while the sun travelled in a slow arc across the sky, we squinted into the middle distance, and the whales did not appear. Even Ali, ever a source of reassurance and inspiration, became withdrawn and quiet, peering about him with one hand shading a furrowed brow. It was with a feeling of disbelief that we found ourselves loading our gear onto the boat on the final day.

After a long day, still no whales had appeared. As the shadows lengthened, a broad, glossy back broke the surface a few hundred yards away. We'd seen this a few times, so didn't get dreadfully excited. Simon and I stirred on the back of the boat, readying snorkels and cameras. We looked at each other grimly. "Last throw of the dice mate", I said. If this whale didn't co-operate, we (and the show) were in desperate trouble.

We slipped off the back of the boat – still about 40m away from the whale – and looked down into the deep water, an absolute rich, dark blue with the suns rays lancing all around us. Deep, deep

Monty and Simon approach the whales on the final dive of the final day.

Simon does his best to creep up on a thirty ton whale in the open ocean.

down, I saw a vague shape, then a touch of white, then a sense of form. It was a tiny humpback, about three weeks old. I hung at the surface, hardly daring to breathe, and gradually it sculled towards me. It ended up about six feet away, peering intently into my face, mystified by this peculiar floating lump of plankton before it.

Looking down again, the water darkened on an altogether more massive scale, and the mother appeared. Rising towards us, she touched the calf with a giant white pectoral, and they both turned away into the blue. They stopped in the middle distance, allowing us to gently fin up alongside them, man and whales studying one another with interest and curiosity. The young whale circled beneath her mother's belly and rose again towards me. Reassured by the huge bulk behind her, she studied me closely, possibly the first human being she had ever encountered. I simply hovered a few metres before her, completely enraptured.

My role in the filming of *Great Ocean Adventures* is to act as the spokesman for our little group, attempting to communicate as best I can the adventures of our small team as we travel the globe. As I clambered back aboard the boat, with Karen already behind the camera, the recording light winking at me as it tracked me to the stern platform, I was in turmoil. There are certain experiences that strike dumb even the most garrulous. All I wanted to do was find a quiet spot in the boat, stare at my feet, and remember the whales. It had been an intensely personal experience, which would feel somehow violated by babbling at a camera.

The humpback calf nestles beneath the immense bulk of a watchful mother.

Nonetheless I chattered away, all the while feeling somewhat detached. Finally the red light was extinguished, and I could at last be alone, with the only the setting sun and the memory of the whale to see me home to the harbour for the final time.

A moment that will
stay with me for the
rest of my life.

Chapter 7

A Shark's Tail

The Philippines

In search of the elusive thresher

A Sharks Tail – In search of the elusive thresher.

Being a firm believer in karma, and having braved the three hour drive up the coast road of Cebu in the Philippines with a driver who obviously also held equally strong views about reincarnation, it all seemed rather apt that the island looming on the distant horizon looked classically beautiful. It had been an exhausting journey, consisting of a tedious succession of flights and then an exhilarating drive along twisting coastal roads. These were filled with snorting multi-coloured buses appearing exuberantly from blind corners, everyone mistaking their horn for their brakes, and the occasional car wreck dotting the side of the road like bizarre modern sculpture. The sun had settled low on the horizon ahead of us as we climbed out of the mini-bus with the glassy-eyed stares of combat veterans, to be transferred to a banca – a local boat fitted with elegantly curved outriggers – for the last leg across the limpid straight of water that divided the mainland from the tiny island of Malapascua.

Previous page
Malapascua Island – the home of the thresher shark.

142

The reason that Malapascua should loom large in any diver's itinerary lurks off the steep sides of Monad Shoal, an undersea mountain several kilometers off its coast. This is the thresher shark capital of the world, a near mythical creature for any diver. It is so rare and elusive that there are very few divers who see a thresher shark in a lifetime's exploration of the oceans. Yet every morning the sharks spiral up out of the deep, dark waters to visit the cleaning stations that dot the lip of this undersea cliff.

The silhouette on the thresher shark is one of the most unmistakable of any animal in the sea, a giant scimitar of a tail pushing a compact body through the water in a series of gentle undulations. This extraordinary tail, the same length as the body, drives the shark forwards whilst the great sweeping pectoral fins trim the body in the horizontal plane, an elegant testimony to millions of years of evolution. Theories differ as to the precise function of the tail: one suggests that it is used to stun fish and even seabirds, another eulogizes its hydrodynamic perfection, and a third maintains that it exists primarily to drive the shark through the surface of the water

A fisherman sculls home as the sun sets behind the island.

Local transport, a one way ticket to oblivion

in a series of spectacular breaches, presenting the heart-stopping sight of a great grey rapier exploding from the middle of the ocean into the light, spreading a glittering shrapnel of spray.

When researching the thresher prior to the trip, certain expressions kept appearing that were a real measure of how this shark has eluded man through the ages. The World Conservation Union, which collates population details for pretty much every animal on earth, records simply that the thresher is "data deficient". In a study of all shark species conducted in 2003 to gauge the appalling carnage being wreaked by the long liners, it was simply noted that "few reliable records are known" about the thresher, and that most images of the shark are taken after it is dead. This shark, perhaps the most graceful and elegant large predator in the ocean, is known to us mainly through still-life images of blood-stained corpses on oily decks, stripped of power and poise, gasping and staring, retaining only a whisper of the symphony of its movement in its former natural environment.

Like a Formula One racing car, the thresher has design features to enable it to explode instantly from idle cruising into a blur of speed that inevitably ends in the death of any fish unwise enough to stray from the protection of the reef. The head is pointed, with a tiny mouth and huge eye – for this is a visual predator that operates in the twilight world of deep water. Man has little to fear from the thresher. The small mouth is adapted a diet that is 97% fish, and gives the animal an almost fox-like appearance. This is reflected in the local names for the thresher around the world – the sea fox, fox shark, and the Loup de Mer. The French, being French, remain unsatisfied with giving the shark just one name, and also refer to it as the faux, and – my personal favourite – the poisson-épée. The absolute biscuit has to go to a Spanish fisherman I once interviewed, who blew out stubbled cheeks when I showed him an image of a thresher, stared into the middle distance with dark eyes that flashed with memories of that remarkable body blasting through the surface miles from shore, and murmured reverentially, "Ahhhhhh.......Zorro!"

The skin of the thresher has a silky grey sheen, like a carefully polished classic car. The final evolutionary nod to extreme speed lies beneath the surface however, in a network of fine capillaries called – in a rare instance of scientific emotion – the *retia mirabilia*, or miraculous net. Like the baffles and filaments of a finely tuned motor, these maintain the sharks body in a perpetual state of warmth, ready for a burst of pace at any moment.

In common with every shark species, threshers are threatened by an almighty co-ordinated assault from man: the quest for fins to feed

145

The thresher shark – the formula one racing car of the sea.

the insatiable markets in the Far East. Unusually that great tail has little value for sharks fin dealers, being considered too gelatinous for soup. Nonetheless any thresher shark caught is quickly broken down into useable parts. As in so many shark species, the giant liver makes up much of the total body weight (10% in the case of the thresher), and its oil is used in cosmetics, health food, and – ironically – engines, the lingering memory of speed parodied in whirring cogs and thrashing pistons.

I finally set foot ashore on Malapascua in complete darkness, and found myself, quite unreasonably, in the foulest of foul moods. We had arrived in complete darkness, and after leaping none too athletically off the brightly coloured bow of the boat, I was soon walking up a white sand beach towards a shadowy set of huts tucked into the luxuriant growth of the island's interior. I started to climb the steps to the bar on the crest of the hill, a gigantic dive bag swinging off one shoulder.

Such foul temper may not actually be all that illogical. There is – of course – a somewhat idyllic image that springs to mind for most people when they imagine a filming trip, particularly a trip such as this involving a relentless series of tropical islands, sun-kissed beaches and crystal clear water. This image is magnified by the end result of all the filming efforts, a neatly cut televison programme, complete with a suitably languid backing track, that sees our hero the presenter mysteriously whisked from place to place and from one breath-taking encounter to another. The reality is much more prosaic, with tight budgets, long days, and an unending series of departure lounges, surly customs officials, bovine check-in staff, and vast piles of bags and crates to be humped from airport to bus to hotel to boat and back again. For the two-minute footage of the presenter stroking a dolphin's flank in the open ocean, piped into the viewers home on a crashing wave of emotionally charged music, there may well have been several hours while that same presenter sat on a loo in a fly-blown hotel, an ashen face greased with sweat illuminated only by a flickering neon sign by the window, as the latest local delicacy thundered exuberantly out of his system. Sadly, the real story of these filming trips is often passed by in favour of the guaranteed money shot, although I can't help thinking occasionally that the story behind the filming itself is infinitely more intriguing than the few moments of footage that make up the end result.

Sooner or later everyone on a film crew, except for the occasional relentless enthusiast (who of course are the most intensely annoying types of all), gets cheesed off at some point. Today it seemed to be my turn, and the rest of the crew gave me a wide berth. Minutes after arrival, my mood was starting to improve slightly as I nursed a large gin and tonic in the bar, warm breezes spinning the wind chimes on the balcony as the waves rustled on the beach below. Just as I began to feel my equilibrium being magically restored, I

A banca rocks at anchor prior to a dawn departure.

became dimly aware that Simon had appeared behind me. His look was distinctly shifty.

"What?" I said, suspicions immediately aroused.

"I've ahhhhh….ahem….sorted out the dives for tomorrow," he said, eyeing the exit with measured interest, "and we're off at 4 a.m." The final words tumbled out and were accompanied by a winning smile and a distinct edging towards the sanctuary of the door.

I stared gloomily into the contents of my glass. That meant only four hours of sleep, followed by a deep dive on the edge of a shoal rising from abyssal depths, searching for one of the most elusive and mysterious of all the sharks. With regret I pushed away my gin and tonic, and ordered a mineral water.

A few hours later, I was fumbling in the dark for the alarm clock and preparing to set out to the dive operation across the other side of the island. We had been assured that this was a mere ten minutes walk away, which quietly ignored the absolute warren of tracks and paths through the tiny fishing villages on the island. This first trip to the dive operator, which began in darkness and ended in the first hint of dawn some time later, was only made possible by the intervention of two tiny children. Finding us crashing, sweating and swearing amongst the pigs and chickens in the darkness at the back of their hut, instead of chasing us off with sticks they

Racing towards the edge of the shoal as the sun rises.

took a hand each and led us to the waiting boat. Mission accomplished, they skipped off to find more tourists. I got the impression this was a distinctly well-worn routine.

The distant horizon was just glowing as the boats moved quietly out to sea. The vessels used for diving of Malapascua are the same traditional bancas that had brought us to the island – with sweeping white prows, curved outriggers and vivid traditional designs covering their hulls. After loading my gear I introduced myself to the crew, the response each time a flash of white teeth and a weary wave – no-one particularly likes 4am, even nuggety ex-fishermen tanned and lined by a lifetime at sea. Having made our introductions, I found a seat at the bow as the vessel came to life beneath me, turning seaward to greet the sun as it emerged from the fire of a distant horizon.

An hour later, we moored at a lone buoy in a seemingly featureless patch of sea. Despite the early hour, we kitted up with pulses racing. Stepping into the sea, there was faint air of unreality to think that in the pitch black of the deep water beneath us, a freakish undulating tail could well be powering a thresher towards our rendezvous at the edge of the reef. We drifted down to the point where the reef plunged vertically into deep water, and settled beside what was plainly an ancient cleaning station. Preparing for a long wait, I looked down to seek out a spot where I could lie for the entire dive without damaging any coral. Settling like some gigantic cuttlefish in a puff of silt and sand, I glanced up and there, about fifteen feet in front of me, was a thresher shark.

I stared dumbstruck for a moment as it swept past, that magnificent tail undulating gently, the huge eye regarding me with what seemed genuine curiosity. Here was the creature of myth and legend made real, an encounter I'd firmly believed would never take place. Gathering what passed as my wits, I turned to see Simon calmly filming me, and began to babble at the camera. The shark dutifully circled us for several minutes, despite my rapidly increasing enthusiasm and volume, even pausing for a swift polish and brush up at the cleaning station before drifting back over the deep water at the edge of the drop off. The sheen of its skin was quite beautiful, with the body beneath barely moving, a compact package of muscle propelled by the huge waving spoiler above it. Finally overcome with curiosity, or perhaps realizing that these peculiar creatures cowering on the reef before it were not a threat, the shark came

in for one final pass, soaring only feet overhead, pectorals like the swept back wings of a fighter aircraft, tail undulating with waves of subtle power. Simon filmed it all, twisting his body to follow the shark as it swept inches above him. Breathtaking footage – the finale of our programme in the first moment of the first dive of the first morning.

After the dive we puttered back to shore, and trudged wearily through thick white sand towards the intoxicating whiff of breakfast. As the coffee was poured and the toast demolished, I glanced at my watch. It was 8 a.m. – and our target animal was already framed, filmed and filed. Some day all wildlife filming will be this way. I reached across and patted Simon on the shoulder, a sheepish apology which he accepted with a grin framed by white cappuccino froth.

Simon descends towards the edge of the shoal.

The first glimpse of the elusive thresher.

There was, of course, a real danger of the rest of the week being a bit of an anti-climax as we had already bagged the star of the show. However, there were two saving graces. The first was that the reefs of the Philippines teem with life, so we had our hands full trying to do them justice in the few days we had remaining. The second thing was the people of Malapascua – the warmest, most gentle, sweet natured people I had ever encountered on any of my travels. There are 7,107 islands in the Philippines archipelago, said by the locals to have been formed when a weary giant dropped a massive rock ball that exploded into thousands of splinters. I'm willing to bet that none of those other rocky shards have more delightful inhabitants than this one.

A simple walk through one of the many fishing villages, with picture-perfect huts lining narrow paths dotted with cockerels, pigs and dogs scratching in the sand, would turn rapidly into a triumphant procession. There are huge numbers of children on the island who are cared for by only one family or central matriarchal figure, the reason being the absence of their parents earning money on the mainland or overseas. As such, great packs

of small brown children would shout in delight as I approached, beaming at me as they skipped alongside, holding my hand and chattering away. I whiled away many minutes playing games with them, feeling for all the world like some friendly giant in their midst, fee-fi-fo-fumming my way after them as they shrieked with laughter, magically crossing age, language and cultural barriers. The adults would wave and smile, sometimes beckoning me to join them in their tiny porch, or simply calling out a greeting as I passed. Groups of men working together to build fishing boats would stop and lean on their tools, smiling a greeting and exchanging small talk. Perhaps it was the nature of this tight-knit fishing community, perhaps the essence of living on an island without a great deal of money and therefore intense reliance on friends and neighbours, but whatever the cause, I never finished any journey around Malapascua without a smile. It was always a fascinating contrast to slip back into the resort and be surrounded by tourists with huge amounts of relative wealth, cocooned in their world and suspicious of those around them, unsmiling and intense. It left me feeling that we have much to learn from simple communities like these.

Ancient meets modern. Diving Philippines style while Simon films in the background.

We turned our attention over the next few days to the reefs that skirt Malapascua. The Philippines sit in the bullseye of what is poetically known by marine biologists as the Triangle of Diversity. This patch of islands and ocean includes Malaysia, Indonesia and the Philippines, and stretches to the eastern edge of the Papua New Guinea. The abundance of life here gets scientists very excited indeed whenever species numbers are discussed in this region. As a measure of just how unique it is, it's worth noting that Japan failed to be included in the triangle in a 2003 study, as it fell just below the 500 species of coral required. To put that in perspective, a typical Caribbean reef has about fifty species of coral, and the Galapagos has thirty one. Estimates vary enormously as to fish species numbers, but even the driest of scientific studies speak in terms of thousands. A fair estimate is at least 2,000, although 3,000 is quoted just as frequently, and one wild-eyed marine biologist cornered me in a bar one evening and speckled me with spittle as he sprayed the words "Six thousand!!" from lips moist with excitement.

The tragedy is that the reefs are subjected to a particularly brutal and barbaric range of fishing techniques. Population pressure has seen a dramatic increase in cyanide and dynamite fishing, as well as *muro ami*, a means of driving fish into nets using rocks bounced along the reef on pieces of rope held by swimmers at the surface. It is hideously destructive of the coral. It is estimated that only 5-10% of coral reefs in the Philippines remain pristine, with the remainder damaged to varying degrees by the activities of man. According to the Nature Conservancy Council, approximately 70% of all coral reefs worldwide will disappear in the next fifty years unless drastic action is taken, and the Philippines represent the front line in what is becoming a desperate battle.

An unlikely gladiator in this struggle is the portly owner of *Paradise Divers* on Malapascua. Dik de Boer is a cliché'd Dutchman – laid back and amiable. On arriving on the island in the early 1990's, Dik was told about the threshers by local fishermen, and judged – quite rightly – that divers would come from round the world for a one-off encounter. His business has grown accordingly, and although the poster boy undoubtedly remains the thresher shark, he has also created a vibrant reef system close to the beach in front of his resort. With nearly twenty years in thePhilippines behind him, he still retained an almost impenetrable Dutch accent.

"I shimply thought that if I schtick things in the shea, the fish would schwim towardsh them." He told me with commendable honesty over a latte (another tremendous innovation he introduced to the island). "I'm no schientisht, but it sheemed logical."

He was quite right, and over the years has gleefully hurled various objects into the shallows off the resort. This is not a random effort though, as he carefully monitors the colonization of these artificial reefs, and leans towards materials that favour colonization. He now has a full-time work shop at the back of the dive operation, producing twisted lumps of metal that become the foundation for coral formation. Such has been the success of his artificial reef programme that local fishing boats now occasionally drift towards it to plunder it, to be chased off with cries of Dutch outrage.

Dik led me to the workshop at the back of the dive operation, where a very large man indeed was sweating in a vest as he wielded a blowtorch to create a sculpture of a thresher shark to be placed within the artificial reef. Between welding, he would bend (large) bits of metal with vast hands, muscles pulsing under mahogany

Simon and Roger chat on the ride home.

shoulders. Lighting the blowtorch was done with the business end of a rolled up cigarette, nonchalantly placed back between his lips before the welder's mask snapped into place. The thresher shark sculpture was an idea – and a very good one too – from the tv company co-ordinating the series in the UK, although I couldn't help feeling that this was lost somewhat on the chap making it. As the cameras whirred, Karen asked me to get stuck in with the blowtorch and add the final touches to the plinth. My resultant ball of weld (or whatever it's called) became the size of an orange and the consistency of old chewing gum. It was regarded with withering disbelief by the vest-wearing, roly-smoking metal bender, and I was quietly shouldered aside. Very soon the sculpture was sat atop its peculiarly shaped plinth as I stood in the background, feeling curiously unmanned by the entire episode.

The sculpture of the thresher shark heads out to sea and a new life as a reef.

157

With the application of a great deal of manpower and shouting, the sculpture was moved down the beach, to be balanced on a small skiff. Having thus created the most unstable boat in the Philippines (and that's up against some pretty stiff competition, believe me), the crew made their wobbly way out to the reef, unceremoniously dumping the sculpture overboard to settle in an cloud of sand on the seabed. Even as the sand cleared, a school of curious batfish sculled over to inspect it, the first residents on a new local tenement that for them had mysteriously dropped from the skies.

Our final dive was to Gato Island, another monument to local conservation efforts. Established as a nature reserve in the late 1990's, it still has problems as illegal fishermen constantly make forays over its delicate reefs, but it is, at least, a bastion of hope in a beleaguered region. Although the reefs are vibrant in themselves, coating a twisting series of volcanic rock formations and honeycombed with tunnels, there is one animal in particular for which the island has become famous: a beautiful, and particularly deadly, sea snake.

The banded sea krait is a very interesting animal indeed, having recently – in evolutionary terms anyway – made the jump from land to sea. This is obvious in its need to breed on shore, and that its land-based diet of other snakes has been seamlessly replaced with a diet of eels in the sea. As an air breathing reptile, it must surface frequently, and makes an alarming sight for speedo- clad snorkelling day-trippers as it barrels out of the deep water beneath them. A level of disquiet is not entirely misplaced, as banded sea kraits are one of the most venomous reptiles on the planet. Its bite delivers 10-15 milligrams of venom, and the first 1.5 milligrams are all that is required to messily kill you – the rest presumably being some form of twisted insurance. Its venom has a potent combination of neurotoxins that attack the nervous system, and myotoxins that simultaneously get on with rotting your skeletal muscles. If bitten you would descend into twitching madness as your flesh sloughed off your bones – it all seems a tad excessive for a small snake that eats eels, if you ask me.

The silky sheen of a thresher's skin is one of its many adaptations for speed.

My dive with the sea snakes was, however, fairly uneventful. As with just about every animal on earth, the appearance of man is a cause to flee rather than attack, and I actually felt rather guilty as I pursued an increasingly annoyed snake over the kaleidoscopic crest of the reef. There was one exhilarating moment as the snake stopped, turned, and gave me an appropriately cold-blooded look before resuming its sinuous progress into the blue, and I duly backed off.

The remarkable tail of the thresher shark.

Malapascua Island is quite beautiful, the experience of diving diverse reefs enhanced by the warmth of the people who wait on shore. The island has much to offer, as is recognized by a burgeoning tourist industry. However despite the attractions above the waves, it is the dark shadow that circles the island off its sloping undersea shoulders that is the true draw. A creature from a Tolkein fantasy that has eluded man for thousands of years – the mysterious thresher shark.

Chapter 8

The Drifting Giant

Bali

The Great Ocean Sunfish

The Drifting Giant – The Great Ocean Sunfish

Bali was the final destination on what had been a truly epic round the world trip, and as such it needed to be a corker. Despite the wonder of all we had experienced, we were knackered, with a faint air of hollow-eyed madness about us. Our cup had run over with unforgettable sights and tremendous encounters, and it was time to go home. Fortunately Bali provided not only the spectacular destination to fan the final glowing embers of our energy, but a suitably explosive encounter to finish our journey in the form of the mola mola, otherwise known as the giant ocean sunfish.

Many years previously, I had studied marine biology at Plymouth University. The final year of my course saw me furiously making up for squandering the previous two years puffing ineffectually around various rugby pitches and drinking gallons of coffee on the sea front. Well aware that I was heading for an ignominious exit from my degree, I decided radical action was required.

Previous page
Fishing boats in the dawn on the island of Nusa Lembongan.

164

On Plymouth Hoe stands the formidable headquarters of the Marine Biological Association. The building has an intimidating grey stone facade that is four-square to the sea front, glowering out over the harbour. It is the citadel for marine biological record keeping and development in the United Kingdom, a fortress of academia where trembling undergraduates like myself are the equivalent of evolutionary sludge (although not quite as interesting).

At the start of my third year, I took one last lingering look at the sun, and then vanished into the dusty halls of the MBA. At the end of one of the corridors, through large ornate doors, is the library – the inner sanctum and depository of the accumulated knowledge of the resident academics for over a hundred years. The library has the whiff of the great Victorian explorers about it, with rows of leather-bound books crammed onto oak shelves, and subdued lighting that doesn't quite reach the darker corners. Here lurk the truly momentous tomes, telling tales of forgotten expeditions and deep sea explorations. A magical collection of tales of the remarkable pioneering days of early marine biology.

Fishing in the shadow of one of the islands volcanoes.

This was very nearly my undoing, as my carefully laid plans for study slipped away between the yellowing pages of these books. I spent many a happy hour opening crumbling reports the size of ping-pong tables and poring over tales told when the sea was considered a cold, dark, echoing hell full of monsters, myths and mermaids.

In the heart of one of the smaller publications – *The Wide World Magazine* of December 1910 – was a sepia-tinted picture of the most extraordinary marine animal I had ever seen. The image showed a group of Australians, frock-coated and top-hatted, standing around a vast monster. A palpable air of shock emanated from the people in the image, crossing almost a hundred years to be reflected in my own wide-eyed gaze, much the same as if a modern group of dock workers came across a dead tyrannosaurus floating in on the tide. There are very few smiles, just a series of looks ranging from bewildered awe to disbelief.

The colossal creature in their midst is a giant ocean sunfish. Very large, and very dead. The day before the photo was taken, on the 18th September 1908, the merchant vessel *SS Fiona* was forty miles off the Australian coast, steaming towards Sydney. These were the days when the ocean was a vital link for the people of Australia, a life-line bringing in stores, food, and news of the outside world. These were serious, ocean-going trade vessels, riveted steel monsters weighing thousands of tons that ploughed the international trade routes across both hemispheres on voyages lasting many months.

Abruptly, in a clear patch of ocean, the vessel slowed by several knots. Despite the best efforts of the skipper, and a substantial increase in power, the *SS Fiona* still remained well below her top speed. The skipper limped his ship the final few miles to Sydney, where the mystery was revealed.

Draped across the bow, still alive and struggling weakly, was a monster from the sea. Its skin was so rough it had removed the paint from the hull, its body so immense that the vessel had been slowed with its weight and drag. Hauled ashore to expire on the dock, the real dimensions were revealed.

Thought to be the largest ocean sunfish on record, this animal weighed 2,300 kg, over two tons. It measured fourteen feet from fin tip to fin tip, and ten feet from mouth to tail. No larger sunfish has ever been caught, and it created a sensation that swept the world. The image mesmerized me, offering what seemed a glimpse of a true sea monster.

It was therefore with an intense sense of anticipation that I sat on the bow of a small boat many years later, approaching the only place where these giants were said to consistently gather in any numbers. We were steaming over the edge of a deep water trench in southern Bali, the greatest sunfish hotspot in the world.

We arrived in the dark at the beautiful island of Nusa Lembongan, and made our weary way ashore. I had lost over a stone in weight over the course of the filming trip, the relentless schedule taking its toll: the subsequent television series will show my progression from "hale and hearty diver just showing a touch of middle aged spread" to "recently released Changi prisoner".

I summoned the strength to visit the bar before going to sleep, walking through the maze of the beautiful thatched huts of the resort under the silver glow of a full moon. The bar was on the beach itself, bathed in the eerie light from the cloudless night sky, with the shadows of local fishing boats rocking gently at their moorings only metres away. The surf folded itself lazily onto the beach and

Nusa Lembongan – a
small slice of paradise.

the warm air carried the scent of the tropical undergrowth that
draped itself on the cliffs at either end of the beach.

This tranquil, timeless scene was a balm to the soul. I quickened
my pace, before being abruptly stopped in my tracks by a bull
bellow from the bar. "Flintoff's a complete pussy!" came a distinctly
Antipodean roar on the night breeze. "You Poms got lucky. We're
just trying to make a contest of it to keep the viewing figures for
the next Ashes series vaguely respectable."

Thus was my introduction to Michael Cortenbach, my guide
for the next week. Entrepeneur, diver, part time biologist, and
full-time, card carrying, professional Australian. Michael was a

blonde, affable and hugely energetic figure in his early forties, and was the pioneer of sunfish diving here in Bali. He had come to Nusa Lembongan in the early nineties as – in his own words – a "bloody awful surfer." Stories had abounded of massive tiger sharks patrolling the line of still water behind the surf, and it was Michael who spotted that the ominously large fins slicing through the surface were, in fact, those of giant sunfish. He had the acumen and guile to realise that he had a world-beating wildlife attraction on his hands, and set up a dive operation to lead people to what he saw was a unique encounter. Fifteen years later, his business empire has expanded, and he now supervises and governs the majority of diving activities with the sunfish.

The special relationship between a presenter and his crew.

Michael waved me over to the stool beside him as he saw me emerge from the darkness. "Hello mate, Michael's the name, welcome to Nusa Lembongan." A beer magically appeared on the bar beside him which he pushed it towards me, before turning back to a slightly stunned looking Simon and Roger to continue his enthusiastic diatribe on the state of England in general, and our sportsman in particular.

Our conversation from that point on revolved around three distinct topics. How England should never have won the Rugby World Cup ("You buggers got lucky"), how England should never have won the Ashes ("You buggers got lucky"), and – eventually – diving with the sunfish.

The locals have very little interest in the sunfish, considering them too oily to eat.

As he explained the latter, the realization dawned that this was a very serious diving proposition indeed. The channel between Nusa Lembongan and the Balinese mainland is said to be the deepest on earth relative to its width – it is only 35km across, but 1300m deep. Funnelling the two great ocean basins at either end, the channel becomes a bottle neck as the tide rises and falls. Billions of tons of water come barreling through the strait, swirling and twisting in huge eddies, roaring over the reefs in an undersea gale, contorting into whirlpools and ferocious currents. The sunfish ride in on these currents – indeed there is speculation that they are designed as underwater kites, turning those huge mottled sides into the prevailing water movement and drifting effortlessly over vast distances.

To see the sunfish it is necessary to dive at exactly the right time, and even then the dives take place at a considerable depth. As the tide stills and the sunfish sweep towards the sides of the channel, it is essential to be sitting beside the cleaning stations that dot the edges of this dark underwater canyon. The cleaning stations are at depths of over 120ft, requiring the correct gear, good diving skills, and a cool head. The latter is not helped by the effects of breathing gas under pressure. At certain depths (it varies for every individual, but below about 100ft very few people will be making a great deal of sense), the air we all breathe becomes narcotic, leading to a very similar sensation to being drunk. I am particularly susceptible to narcosis, and have had some entertaining episodes on deep dives in the past. The effect of what is essentially a giant floating head appearing out of the gloom as I hung off the side of an abyssal canyon being swept by an undersea gale would only be known when it happened, but it certainly had the potential to be extremely exciting for not only myself but also my dive buddies. With this exhilarating prospect in mind, I made my excuses and began the rather thoughtful journey back to my beach hut, head spinning with images of the gigantic animal that awaited me the next day.

The sunfish is one of the great mythical creatures of the sea. Sighted by incredulous lookouts perched in swaying crow's nests over the years, or glimpsed in the open ocean by terrified indigenous fishermen, it was named the sunfish due to its habit of basking on its side at the water's surface. The truth behind this behaviour is even more remarkable than the myth – the sunfish is actually thought to lie in this position on the surface so that seagulls can peck parasites from its vast expanse of skin. There is no shortage of prey to be found there for the gulls, as the sunfish plays host to more marine parasites than any other fish in the sea. Such is the abundance of the various communities that scuttle, slither and crawl over its skin, that when a sunfish appears at a cleaning station on a reef, up to six separate smaller fish species will browse over it like some floating buffet. It drifts through the oceans as a huge mother ship, manned by a crew of parasites that live, breed and die on the great plains of its skin.

The sunfish is also known as the Mola Mola, from the Latin name for a millstone. One glance at the animal shows how the name originated, but begs all manner of questions as to the need for such a bizarre piece of design. The sunfish comes from the same order as trigger fish and puffer fish, using the same twin-finned design to scull itself gently through the water. Instead of a tail, the sunfish has a clavus, a flattened rear end used more as a rudder than a means of propulsion. Controlling that huge disc of a body requires more subtle trimming techniques, and the sunfish uses jets of water from its mouth and gills to make small adjustments in direction and position, for all the world like a space ship maneuvering with booster rockets.

The skin is over an inch thick, and covered in glutinous slime. The mouth is fused to form a beak, hence the name of the order from which it stems – the tetradontiformes. The sunfish sculls through the oceans investigating – and if possible eating – anything vaguely planktonic that crosses its path. In turn it has very few predators. Man does not actively pursue the sunfish, the flesh being considered too oily to eat. Great whites and orcas will occasionally take the adults, although such behaviour is not thought to be common. Californian sea lions will attack the juveniles, with numerous reports of them using the sunfish as frisbees, tossing them to one another on the surface. In these circumstances the sunfish – I imagine – dies more of shame than anything else.

The sunfish produces more eggs than any other vertebrate on earth - around 300 million. Each larva is only a tenth of an inch long, with the subsequent growth the equivalent of a human baby growing up to weigh the same as five Titanics. The lifestyle of this animal – sculling through the wilderness of the open ocean, unmolested by man – means that scientists still know very little about it.

After a restless night filled with dreams of hurtling into darkness, limbs pinwheeling wildly whilst surrounded by massive heads laughing hysterically, I was amazed at the surge of strength that greeted the dawn. The sun revealed a white sand beach in front of my hut, some very nice looking surf, and – the final piece of the jigsaw - several even nicer looking girls overlooking the beach, eating their breakfast on the large veranda. This was too much to bear, and I immediately skipped onto the sand, tucked a handy surf-ski under one arm, and bounded in the approved fashion to the waters edge. Hurling the surf-ski into the water, I leapt aboard and flailed away with the paddle, racing out to meet the first oncoming wave. I'd love to say this wave was a great crackling monster, but actually it would have come half way up a hobbit's hairy shin. Nonetheless, it had enough of a physical and psychological impact when it arrived to cause me to flail and turn turtle with impressive speed. As my naked back smacked meatily into the water, I recalled with crystal clarity that the only two surf sites I could name in Bali were called "Laceration" and "Surgery". A wild-eyed peer sideways revealed the staghorn coral awaiting my hurtling torso just beneath the surface, and there was the powerful conviction that this really was going to hurt. A lot.

It did. I staggered out of the water bleeding impressively, every croissant paused half way to open mouth on the veranda. The wounds had to be dabbed with alcohol by a tittering Alastair, whilst

I squirmed and gasped on a sun bed. The only consolation was the impressive collection of scars that I insisted be incorporated into the show, and were duly filmed from all angles over the next few days.

It was time to head off to the dive vessel. With impressive punctuality for this part of the world, it nosed onto the beach precisely on time. The vessel was a garish yellow and blue hardboat, a collection of steel plates and strengthened glass. It looked completely invincible, like a compact seaborne tank, having been built to cope with the potent local mix of unpredictable currents and uncharted reefs.

Once Michael had recovered from the helpless mirth engendered by the lattice work of weeping scars on my back ("Mate, Poms really shouldn't surf, although it is a good chance for them to have a wash"), he briefed us in detail about the dive ahead. The boat would be held in position in the teeth of the current by the wall of the channel. Michael would look over the side using a mask and snorkel, and providing not too many fish were going past upside down and backwards, it would be okay to dive. "We can't mess about here fellas" he said, serious for a moment, "we have to get to the wall and get to the lee of the cleaning stations. We do not want to get caught in a down current."

In 1995, Michael and his dive buddy had been pinned under a ledge for twenty five minutes by a down current, like climbers on a Himalayan ridge. Only a monumental effort had seen them clamber and claw their way back up the reef to safety. Over the years other divers had not been quite so lucky, and Michael was now keenly attuned to diving responsibly in this unpredictable terrain, the marine equivalent of a wind tunnel.

It was therefore a reasonably subdued group that kitted up over the channel, the boat's engines muttering behind us, holding the vessel in position. Michael was lying on the stern platform, face in the water, muttering through a snorkel with an unmistakably Aussie twang. Lifting his head from the water, he looked at the expectant faces around him. "Right lads, we're on." I secured the final few pieces of gear with fingers that fumbled and slipped, unnecessarily tightening straps and repeatedly checking buckles.

Simon, Monty and Roger ready to go. The very last dive of the series.

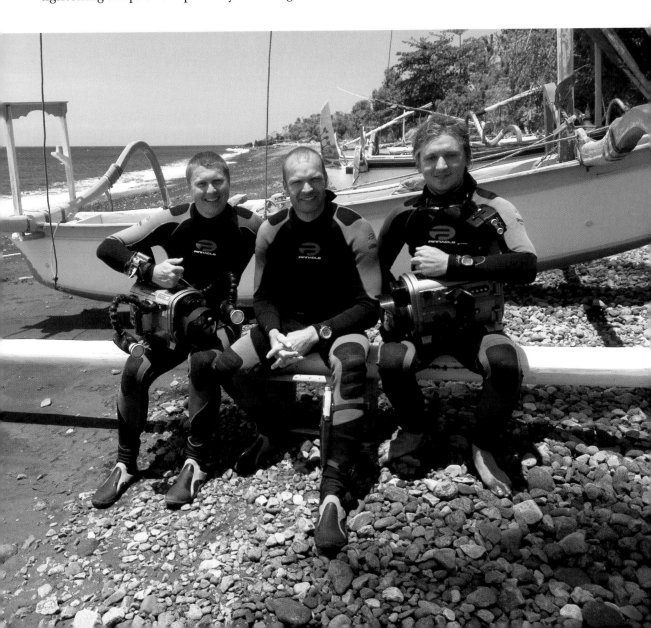

Monty and Roger hang on the edge of the canyon and circle a giant.

Once in the water, we finned hard towards the walls of the channel, appearing like a great undulating cliff faces out of the blue. It was, however, a cliff face on a conveyor belt, moving past us as we slipped sideways with the current. The reassuring form of Michael was ahead of us, angling into one of the dark ridges ahead, and dropping into the lee to look up and wave us down. I angled my body and kicked hard, fuelled by adrenaline, soaring over his head

and twisting like a buzzard in a thermal, keeping low to the reef as I drove back towards him.

Crouched in the lee of the ridge, I saw Simon and Roger swoop in from the blue water beyond the reef, cameras held before them and legs scissoring furiously, their progress marked by streams of bubbles as they worked hard in the teeth of the current. Simon dropped in beside me, and gave me a brief look with a raised laconic eyebrow behind his mask. Looking behind us, we saw Roger alight on the reef and begin to work his way steadily downwards towards the first cleaning station.

Michael led the way as we pushed deeper down the precipitous slope. I was concentrating so hard on keeping pace with him, that I didn't see him frantically pointing ahead. It was a strangled squeak of excitement that made me finally look up – and there ahead of us, suspended over a cleaning station, was the immense form of a giant ocean sunfish.

Simon moves in for a close up.

When one's brain is addled by narcosis, most fish look faintly odd, but in this case the effect was multiplied ten-fold. The massive body was angled slightly towards the surface, brightly coloured banner fish moving over it, picking at lice and flakes of loose skin. The eyes were half closed, almost in ecstasy, and the beak-like mouth gently opened and closed.

Sunfish rely upon their great size for security, and I had been told that, if approached cautiously, they would be quite tolerant of our presence. We crept forward, respectfully timid in the presence of a true giant, and – after a brief dismissive glance – the sunfish resumed its sleepy pose as its multi-coloured courtiers continued to fuss around and over that great expanse of mottled skin.

We were within a few feet of the sunfish when I heard another muffled shriek from Michael. Following his outstretched finger, I saw in the dark gloom of the distant reef slope, another sunfish, and another, and deeper still yet another. We were at the top end of a rank of these huge animals, and the feeling was that of an industrial shipyard, as great tankers dock to be tended by a bustling workforce of uniformed attendants.

We were already very deep indeed – around 150ft, right on the safe limits for diving and filming. To venture deeper could have created some very serious problems in the big currents that surrounded us. Simon was circling the nearest sunfish, pirouetting behind his camera, his body dwarfed by his subject, whilst Roger filmed overhead. Time slowed as the three of us slowly circled this gigantic animal, until abruptly it roused itself, shaking off the bannerfish and coming to life. With a sweep of those two great fins it righted itself and moved with startling speed into the main channel, to be caught by the current and carried away. As quickly as the encounter

had begun, it was over, with our computers chirping at us in an unequivocal message that it was time to leave the sunfish's world and head back to our own.

The boat was quiet as we steamed back to the resort, all of us wrapped in our own thoughts and memories of our final great encounter. The sea had given us a great deal over the last three months, and this was perhaps a time for reflection before the long journey back to England began. It seemed to me that no matter how much intense planning and preparation goes into a trip, how many hours are spent poring over research notes, and how many experts are consulted, you still need luck. We had been a lucky crew, with so many vast dark shadows drifting out of the open ocean around the world to investigate us. The memories of such encounters will last a lifetime.

Face to face with one of the sea's most enigmatic and mysterious creatures.

Appendix 1 – Hosting Organisations

Newfoundland
Ocean Quest Adventure Resort
Conception Bay South, Newfoundland
T: +1 709 834 7234
steve@oceanquestcharters.com

Brazil
(Laguna)
WhaleWatch Operator
Pousada Vida, Sol e Mar (TBC)
Contact: Enrique Litman
Imbituba – SC – Brasil
T : + 55(48) 3355 6111
E: elitman@terra.com.br
www.vidasolemar.com.br

(Fernando de Noronha) – A particular thanks
to the wonderful Lea Zagury, who pretty
much salvaged the whole show for us with her
diplomacy and generosity.

Aguas Claras
Fernando de Noronha, Brazil.
T: +55 81 361 91 225
F: +55 81 361 91 225
Contact: Renato
renato@aguasclaras-fn.com.br
www.aguasclaras-fn.com.br

Norway
Xo Holidays
www.xoholidays.com
Tel: 0870 486 7580
Contact: Asgeir Solli

Mexico
Club Cantamar
Fernando Aguilar
Alvaro Obregon 1665-2
La Paz
Baja California Sur
www.clubcantamar.com

Dolphin Dive Centre
Ave. Benito Juarez
Between Calle Davis and Lopez Mateo
(Malecon)
Loreto, B.C.S. Mexico 23880
Tel: 626-484-9408
www.dolphindivebaja.com

British Colombia
Vancouver Island Dive
Port Hardy, Vancouver Island
Contact: John DeBoeck
40 miles from Telegraph
T: +1 250 753 3751
hideaway@vancouverislanddive.com

Tide Rip Grizzly Tours
Contact: Howard Pattinson
Nr. Knight Inlet (Nr. Vancouver Island)
http://www.tiderip.com/
T: +1 (250) 339-5320 toll free
1-888-643-9319
F: (250) 339-6294
E: tiderip@island.net

Scotland

Silver Swift
Raraig House
Raeric Road
Tobermory
Isle of Mull
Argyll PA75 6PU
Telephone +44 (0) 1688 302 390
Fax +44 (0) 1688 302 391
www.silverswift.co.uk

Tonga

Dolphin Pacific Diving (Dive operator)
Contact: Al Coldrick
Vava'u, Tonga
www.dolphinpacificdiving.com

Philippines

Exotic Dive and Beach Resort
Malapascua Island
Cebu
Philippines
www.malapascua.net/

Bali

Bali Hai Diving Adventures.
Contact: Micheal Cortenbach
(Managing Director)
www.scubali.com
diverse@indosat.net.id
Tel + 62 (0) 361 724 062 / 720331 ext 40
Fax + 62 (0) 361 724 814 / 720334

Appendix 2 – Photographers

Once again, many thanks to the photographers for their images for this book. They are:

Jason Isley
Pages 18/19, 33, 36, 37, 43, 46, 48, 53, 57, 60, 74, 75, 80/81, 84, 90, 96.

Simon Enderby
Pages 16, 20, 34, 38, 40/41, 47, 49, 55, 58, 83, 85, 87, 166, 167,168

Roger Munns
160, 162/163, 174/175, 176, 178/179

Dan Burton
Front cover main image, 109, 111, 116, 117, 118, 119

Dan Stephenson
102, 104/105, 106, 114

Alastair Blane
27, 29, 68, 173

Karen Walsh
30, 50, 66, 95.

Jordi Chias
Front cover x 2, 78, 91, 99, 98/99.

Matthew Oldfield
Front cover x 2

Scott Tuason
Front cover, Back cover, 138, 139

Alfredo Barroso
77